I0408122

NEW ORLEANS: HOW THE CRESCENT CITY BECAME A SANCTUARY CITY

HEARING

BEFORE THE

SUBCOMMITTEE ON IMMIGRATION AND BORDER SECURITY

OF THE

COMMITTEE ON THE JUDICIARY

HOUSE OF REPRESENTATIVES

ONE HUNDRED FOURTEENTH CONGRESS

FIRST SESSION

SEPTEMBER 27, 2016

Serial No. 114–96

Printed for the use of the Committee on the Judiciary

Available via the World Wide Web: http://judiciary.house.gov

U.S. GOVERNMENT PUBLISHING OFFICE

22–124 PDF   WASHINGTON : 2015

COMMITTEE ON THE JUDICIARY

BOB GOODLATTE, Virginia, *Chairman*

F. JAMES SENSENBRENNER, JR.,
   Wisconsin
LAMAR S. SMITH, Texas
STEVE CHABOT, Ohio
DARRELL E. ISSA, California
J. RANDY FORBES, Virginia
STEVE KING, Iowa
TRENT FRANKS, Arizona
LOUIE GOHMERT, Texas
JIM JORDAN, Ohio
TED POE, Texas
JASON CHAFFETZ, Utah
TOM MARINO, Pennsylvania
TREY GOWDY, South Carolina
RAUL LABRADOR, Idaho
BLAKE FARENTHOLD, Texas
DOUG COLLINS, Georgia
RON DeSANTIS, Florida
MIMI WALTERS, California
KEN BUCK, Colorado
JOHN RATCLIFFE, Texas
DAVE TROTT, Michigan
MIKE BISHOP, Michigan

JOHN CONYERS, JR., Michigan
JERROLD NADLER, New York
ZOE LOFGREN, California
SHEILA JACKSON LEE, Texas
STEVE COHEN, Tennessee
HENRY C. "HANK" JOHNSON, JR.,
   Georgia
PEDRO R. PIERLUISI, Puerto Rico
JUDY CHU, California
TED DEUTCH, Florida
LUIS V. GUTIERREZ, Illinois
KAREN BASS, California
CEDRIC RICHMOND, Louisiana
SUZAN DelBENE, Washington
HAKEEM JEFFRIES, New York
DAVID N. CICILLINE, Rhode Island
SCOTT PETERS, California

SHELLEY HUSBAND, *Chief of Staff & General Counsel*
PERRY APELBAUM, *Minority Staff Director & Chief Counsel*

————

SUBCOMMITTEE ON IMMIGRATION AND BORDER SECURITY

TREY GOWDY, South Carolina, *Chairman*
RAUL LABRADOR, Idaho, *Vice-Chairman*

LAMAR S. SMITH, Texas
STEVE KING, Iowa
KEN BUCK, Colorado
JOHN RATCLIFFE, Texas
DAVE TROTT, Michigan

ZOE LOFGREN, California
LUIS V. GUTIERREZ, Illinois
SHEILA JACKSON LEE, Texas
PEDRO R. PIERLUISI, Puerto Rico

GEORGE FISHMAN, *Chief Counsel*
TOM JAWETZ, *Minority Counsel*

(II)

CONTENTS

SEPTEMBER 27, 2016

Page

OPENING STATEMENTS

WITNESSES

OFFICIAL HEARING RECORD

UNPRINTED MATERIAL SUBMITTED FOR THE HEARING RECORD

Material submitted by the Honorable Sheila Jackson Lee, a Representative in Congress from the State of Texas, and Member, Subcommittee on Immigration and Border Security. This material is available at the Subcommittee and can also be accessed at:

http://docs.house.gov/Committee/Calendar/ByEvent.aspx?EventID=105392

NEW ORLEANS: HOW THE CRESCENT CITY BECAME A SANCTUARY CITY

TUESDAY, SEPTEMBER 27, 2016

House of Representatives

Subcommittee on Immigration and Border Security

Committee on the Judiciary

Washington, DC.

The Subcommittee met, pursuant to call, at 10:07 a.m., in room 2141, Rayburn House Office Building, the Honorable Trey Gowdy (Chairman of the Subcommittee) presiding.

Present: Representatives Gowdy, Goodlatte, Labrador, Smith, King, Buck, Ratcliffe, Lofgren, Conyers, and Jackson Lee.

Also Present: Representative Richmond.

Staff Present: (Majority) George Fishman, Chief Counsel; Tanner Black, Clerk; and (Minority) Gary Merson, DHS Detailee.

Mr. GOWDY. Good morning. Welcome. The Subcommittee on Immigration and Border Security will come to order.

Without objection, the Chair is authorized to declare recesses of the Committee at any time. We welcome everyone to today's hearing, entitled New Orleans: How the Crescent City Became a Sanctuary City.

I will recognize myself for an opening statement and then my friend from California. I will introduce the panelists en banc and then recognize you individually for your opening statements.

It is as close as I will ever come to being a judge, but there we have it.

Time and time and time again, our Nation has witnessed the tragic consequences of this Administration's failure to enforce immigration law. Witnessing these tragedies is unsettling enough, but it pales in comparison to the grief and the anguish and the separation experienced by the families of those victimized.

But, today, we are not here merely to discuss the failure to enforce the law. It is even more disconcerting than that. We are here today because the Department of Justice, the entity that is supposed to be the chief enforcer of the law, is aiding and abetting local governments in the failure to enforce the law. Once again, the temptation to make a political point has transcended the obligation to take care that the law be faithfully executed.

Under current policy, the New Orleans Police Department prevents its officers and employees from communicating with U.S. Immigration and Customs Enforcement regarding the immigration status of an arrestee.

In May of 2010, New Orleans Mayor Mitchell Landrieu sent a letter to then Attorney General Holder requesting DOJ "transform the New Orleans Police Department." Based on the Department of Justice report, current Labor Secretary, then Civil Rights Division head, Thomas Perez, filed a lawsuit against the city of New Orleans and the police department alleging various civil rights violations.

On the basis of that lawsuit, the parties entered into a consent decree in 2012, which was approved by a Federal court in 2013. This consent decree stated the New Orleans Police Department officers, "shall not take law enforcement action on the basis of actual or perceived immigration status, including the initiation of stops or other field contacts."

Now, let me read the salient part of that again: Police officers shall not take law enforcement action on the basis of actual immigration status.

And on February 28, 2016, New Orleans Police Department issued a written policy, entitled "Immigration Status," which, number one, prohibits officers from inquiring about an individual's immigration status; number two, prohibits officers from assisting or supporting ICE'S immigration enforcement; and number three, mandates any ICE request for support or assistance be declined.

The New Orleans Police Department policy was not only vetted but, "enthusiastically" approved and supported by DOJ's Civil Rights Division. It was also reviewed and approved by DHS. The Department of Justice and Department of Homeland Security enthusiastically approve and support failure of law enforcement to take note of Federal immigration laws.

In addition to being mind-numbingly antithetical to the faithful execution of the law, which is among the primary responsibilities of the executive branch, this New Orleans policy statement appears to violate section 8 U.S.C. code, 1373, which provides no person or agency may prohibit or restrict a Federal, State, or local agency from sending, requesting, receiving, or exchanging information with ICE regarding unlawfully present aliens.

On May 28 of this year, Chairman Goodlatte sent a letter to now Attorney General Lynch demanding that she explain DOJ's role in initiating litigation against the city of New Orleans and the resulting consent decree and provide the legal justification for approving the sanctuary policies enacted by the police department.

On May 31 of this year, DOJ Inspector General Michael Horowitz issued a memo to the Assistant Attorney General for Justice Programs in response to a request to investigate allegations that over 140 State and local jurisdictions received DOJ grant funds, and they may be in violation of Federal law. Specifically, the inspector general was requested to investigate allegations of the 140 jurisdictions who are recipients of funding from the Department of Justice are in violation of title 8 U.S.C., section 1373.

For those of you who may be struck by the duplicity of the chief Federal law enforcement entity providing grant money to State and municipalities who specifically fail to assist in the enforcement of Federal law, you are not alone. The inspector general found the laws and policies in several jurisdictions go beyond regulating responses to ICE detainers and also address, in some way, the sharing of information with Federal immigration authorities.

After specifically reviewing the language of the New Orleans Police Department policy, the inspector general found, and I quote: In our view, subsection (a) of the NOPD policy would not serve as a 'savings clause' in addressing section 1373. Thus, unless the understanding of NOPD's employees is that they are not prohibited or restricted from sharing immigration status information with ICE, the policy would be inconsistent with Section 1373.''

On July 7, DOJ's Office of Justice Programs determined section 1373 is, ''an applicable Federal law for purposes of determining statutory eligibility for relevant DOJ grant funding.'' Yet despite the requirement of section 1373, DOJ awarded the police department of New Orleans approximately $2 million in grants for fiscal year 2015.

That very same day, July 7, DOJ responded to Chairman Goodlatte's letter. They outlined the policy, but they failed to explain how the New Orleans' policies are lawful, which was a pretty important part of the letter in the first place.

Then, last Friday—last Friday—September 23, just a few days after our hearing was announced, we received a letter from the Department of Justice claiming the revised policy the New Orleans Police Department had issued did comply with 1373. However, this revised policy makes no mention of part B of section 1373. And in addition, DOJ has not provided this Committee with any indication of how officers will be trained to implement this revised policy or how seemingly minor changes to the text will ensure New Orleans will not be operating as a sanctuary city, which leads us to why we are here today.

Not only does this place ICE agents and officers at greater risk when they are forced to arrest criminal aliens who are no longer in a secure jail facility, but instead, in public places, where they can more readily escape or access a weapon, but it also prevents officers from accomplishing their ultimate goal, which is public safety. We already know there are cities more interested in providing sanctuary for criminals than safe haven for our very own citizens. We know there are cities who clamor for the Federal Government to assert itself into matters that are not inherently Federal in nature but refuse to assist Federal law enforcement in matters that actually are inherently Federal.

And to put this in terms that almost anyone can understand, State and local law enforcement can be trusted to provide security for Members of Congress both here and in our home districts. They can be entrusted to enforce murder laws, child sex laws, kidnapping laws. They can participate in Federal task forces on terrorism and narcotics trafficking, but God forbid they lift a finger to assist in the enforcement of Federal immigration laws.

But for the Department of Justice to go as far to seek a consent decree to actually inhibit the ability of the Federal Government to enforce Federal law is stunning, even for a Department of Justice that has, unfortunately, become increasingly politicized. The consent decree can be interpreted to require New Orleans adopt policies that require its officers to actually violate Federal law.

Let me repeat that one more time: This Administration's Department of Justice is actually requiring New Orleans police officers to break the law in an effort to further their political agenda.

We have had multiple hearings on those that have been victimized by sanctuary cities. We have heard from their families. We are well aware of the tragic consequences. This is not a theoretical conversation in some law school conference room. This is real life with real victims and real grieving family members. Illegal immigration is not a victimless crime.

Once you weaken the law, you weaken it forever, and once you put politics above the blind application of the law, it is done forever. And once you decide State and local law enforcement are good enough to protect us when we are back home in our districts but not good enough to be trusted to assist in the execution of the law, good luck in reversing that.

With that, I would recognize the gentlelady from California.

Ms. LOFGREN. Thank you, Mr. Chairman. Today, we are again devoting time to what the majority calls sanctuary cities. It is ironic that my Republican colleagues today argue against local policies in favor of a top-down mandate from Washington. It is a question why the majority believes that it knows better than several hundred State and local police departments across the country that have embraced community trust policing policies precisely because they believe that approach makes us all safer. And for the Republicans to question the need for good community policing approaches at this moment, when reports of tragic police shootings dominate the news, seems nonsensical.

The fact is we could have addressed the Republican concerns with sanctuary cities and many other immigration matters if we had devoted time spent on polemics and diversions instead of to fixing our broken immigration system through comprehensive reform.

When it comes to so-called sanctuary cities, this is what Richard Biehl, the police chief of Dayton, Ohio, not a place many think of as a sanctuary city, said over a year ago, when he testified before the Judiciary Committee, ''These policies allow us to focus our limited resources on our primary mission, crime solving and community safety. They also send a message that victims of violent crime, human trafficking, and other crime should never be afraid to reach out for help due to fear of the immigration consequences.''

I note that in the Department of Justice report investigating the New Orleans Police Department dated March 16, 2011, it said, ''Minority groups nearly uniformly said that the police rarely reach out to them for any purpose.'' One member of a Vietnamese community organization reported that, ''A lot of young Vietnamese people who get shot in this community, we know who shot them, but the New Orleans police won't do anything. They don't talk to us. They don't build community relationships.''

I agree with Chief Biehl, and I know from my experience as a county supervisor and Member of Congress that law enforcement and local officials can work cooperatively with community groups and the Federal Government to come to a consensus position that preserves community policing and prioritizes serious criminals for immigration enforcement and removal.

I also agree with Secretary Johnson's prior statements to this Committee that imposing Federal mandates on local law enforcement by withholding funds would be a huge setback in efforts to improve the relationship between DHS, State, and local law enforcement, and communities around the country.

With respect to New Orleans, the context, like most things in the Big Easy, is a little bit different. Upon taking office, Mayor Landrieu requested the Department of Justice Civil Rights Division engage in a review of the police department. He recognized that a history of civil rights violations by the New Orleans Police Department had undermined trust with the community and reform was necessary.

Of course, the vast majority of New Orleans Police Department officers honestly and conscientiously performed and continued to perform their duties. But I hope that my Republican colleagues are not here to defend the actions of a few that caused such great harm over the years in New Orleans.

The history of abuse by the department has been well documented. The facts are incontrovertible. Under Mayor Landrieu and Superintendent of Police Michael Harrison with the support of the Department of Justice and working with the local community, New Orleans entered into a consent decree and has adopted a bias-free policing policy. The policy ensures that immigrants can report crimes and serve as witnesses without retribution. It also makes clear that information regarding the citizenship and immigration status will be shared with Federal immigration authorities when required by Federal or State law.

Out of an abundance of caution, New Orleans has been working with the Justice Department to revise this language to guarantee its compliance with applicable Federal laws. We now have this revised policy in place. These policies, while not self-identified as sanctuary city polices, are examples of smart, effective community policing tailored by and for the communities in New Orleans.

Many are hopeful that this hard work, done collaboratively with the department and community groups, sets New Orleans on a path to safer streets and better police relations with citizens of all backgrounds. But here comes the Republican Congress to the rescue. They are questioning the legality of a policy that has already been revised to ensure that it is in compliance with Federal law.

Members who have had nothing to do with New Orleans are here to tell the local police and civil leaders how to do their job, even though the New Orleans Police Department says the Republican approach will undermine public safety and make their jobs harder. They are pursuing a line of argument that jeopardizes critical funding, which supports public safety, community policing, and crimes victims services.

With all due respect, I say to my colleagues on the other side of the aisle: let's let local law enforcement and the elected officials in city government do their job, and we should focus on ours. In this Congress, we have gone to the floor to vote on bills to deport DREAMers, to deport the parents of U.S. citizens, to deport vulnerable children fleeing persecution and sex trafficking, and to halt refugee processing amidst the civil war in Syria that has displaced millions.

Thankfully, these proposals have ultimately gone nowhere, but we had the votes to pass comprehensive immigration in the last Congress. The bipartisan bill passed in 2013 would not only have grown our economy, help to shrink our budget deficit; it would have made our communities safer. Bringing people out of shadows and putting them on a path to citizenship would have further enhanced public safety.

If the Republican leadership had given comprehensive immigration reform the same opportunity for a vote that all of these other measures have received, it would be the law today. So let's do the people's business, work to pass immigration reform, and I thank the Chairman.

I yield back the balance of my time.

Mr. GOWDY. The gentlelady yields back.

The Chair will now recognize the gentleman from Virginia, the Chairman of the full Committee, Mr. Goodlatte.

Mr. GOODLATTE. Thank you, Mr. Chairman, and thank you for holding this important hearing.

Sanctuary cities refuse to cooperate with U.S. Immigration and Customs Enforcement in its enforcement of Federal immigration laws. The proliferation of sanctuary cities has resulted in thousands of criminal aliens being released into our neighborhoods to commit more crimes. Sanctuary cities violate Federal law. Two decades ago, Congress enacted a provision, title 8, section 1373, designed specifically to prevent jurisdictions from enacting policies that prohibit their employees from sharing information with ICE about illegally present or criminal aliens.

There are more than 300 sanctuary jurisdictions in the United States. One of these is the city of New Orleans. In 2010, the current major of New Orleans invited the Department of Justice to review the policies of the New Orleans Police Department, apparently in part to transform New Orleans into a sanctuary city. Former Attorney General Eric Holder, former Assistant Attorney General for the Civil Rights Division Thomas Perez, now Secretary of Labor, and the mayor appear to have colluded to have the Department of Justice file a lawsuit against the city, and then have DOJ and the city enter into a settlement agreement or a consent decree that would forbid the New Orleans Police Department from cooperating with ICE.

The resulting consent decree actually required the New Orleans Police Department to develop a plan that prohibited officers from taking any enforcement action based on an individual's immigration status. In February of this year, pursuant to the consent decree, the New Orleans Police Department issued a policy prohibiting officers from inquiring about an individual's immigration status.

More troubling, it generally prohibited officers from assisting or supporting ICE'S immigration enforcement, and it required officers to decline all ICE requests for support or assistance. Thus, New Orleans could claim that DOJ's heavy hand forced it to become a sanctuary city and endanger its residents when in fact it was a willing participant.

The consent decree was a shocking action on the part of the Department of Justice. The chief law enforcement agency of the Federal Government acted to impede the enforcement of Federal law. In addition, the policy appears to be in direct violation of section 1373. Yet it was—excuse me. Yet it was reviewed and approved in advance by the Department of Justice Civil Rights Division. This appears to be another example of the current DOJ's cavalier disregard for the Constitution and the law.

Chairman Gowdy and I sent a letter to the attorney general in May asking that she explain how the New Orleans Police Department policy complies with section 1373 and requesting that she provide communications with New Orleans concerning the development of the policy. DOJ's response was almost completely nonresponsive.

The DOJ inspector general issued a report in May that expressed concern that ambiguous language in some sanctuary policies may cause local officers to comply with such policies in a way that would violate section 1373. The inspector general noted that, ''unless the understanding of New Orleans Police Department's employees is that they are not prohibited or restricted from sharing immigration status with ICE, the policy would be inconsistent with section 1373.'' I have asked for the training materials that the New Orleans Police Department gave to its officers to ensure their understanding of section 1373. I have been provided with nothing.

This leads to a troubling possibility that, through a lack of training, the New Orleans Police Department has, in practice, violated section 1373.

Finally, just 4 days before this hearing, after this Committee's persistent efforts to expose this disturbing matter and demand action, the Department of Justice informed the Committee that the New Orleans Police Department had revised its sanctuary policy.

Specifically, the NOPD policy now states that it is to be construed in accordance with section 1373(a). On that basis, DOJ has represented to the Federal court and this Committee that the policy now complies with section 1373.

Unfortunately, this coordinated effort by DOJ and the city of New Orleans to preserve the patina of legality of their consent decree clearly fails. Section 1373(b) prohibits jurisdictions from restricting their employees from requesting information from ICE, maintaining such information, and exchanging information with other agencies. Nowhere does the revised policy require compliance with this subsection.

A NOPD officer that arrests an individual who is believed to be illegally present is most likely going to contact ICE to request information regarding that individual's immigration status. However, the revised NOPD policy expressly prohibits the New Orleans Police Department officers from making inquiries into an individual's immigration status. DOJ and NOPD have provided no evidence that NOPD, in practice, has complied with section 1373.

They have provided no training material showing that officers have or will be properly trained regarding compliance with section 1373.

The New Orleans Police Department received over $2 million in law enforcement grants from the Department of Justice in fiscal year 2015. As Attorney General Lynch has essentially admitted to John Culberson, Chairman of House Appropriation Committee's

Subcommittee with jurisdiction over the Department of Justice, if the New Orleans Police Department is in violation of section 1373, it would be disqualified from receiving these grants.

Yet the Department of Justice has made no effort to cut off grants to New Orleans. Even aside from the likely violation of Federal law, the Department of Justice's actions in this case show that the protection of our constituents and the enforcement of Federal law no longer seem to be priorities of the Department. In fact, the Department of Justice seems to view them as roadblocks impeding its chosen policy preferences.

I want to thank our witnesses for appearing today, and I look forward to their testimony and to learning more about how this new New Orleans Police Department policy, including why it still prohibits compliance with section 1373(b).

Thank you, Mr. Chairman.

Mr. GOWDY. The gentleman from Virginia yields back.

The Chair will now recognize the gentleman from Michigan, the Ranking Member of the full Committee, Mr. Conyers.

Mr. CONYERS. Thank you, Chairman Gowdy, and I join in welcoming all of our witnesses. I would like to preface my remarks regarding today's hearing, which deals with community policing policies by observing that our Nation's conscience continue to be rocked by a series of tragic events involving law enforcement and the loss of too many Black lives. In our courtrooms, in our streets and on television, we confront a never-ending body count.

Earlier this summer, my congressional colleagues and I staged an unprecedented sit-in just to try to get a vote on commonsense gun legislation. In this Committee, Chairman Goodlatte and I formed a bipartisan policing strategies working group to begin examining how we can best ensure that Congress takes responsibility for the conversation about race and policing in America.

I believe this working group is one of the best examples of how we can come together at a time when the Nation needs our leadership to reduce the levels of violence in our communities. And just this past week, I joined my Congressional Black Caucus colleagues in protest of yet another series of senseless killings of Black men and Black children by police in Cleveland, Tulsa, and Charlotte.

When you add to this volatile mix the attacks on the police officers in Baton Rouge and Dallas, the Nation risks being forced into a battle of whose lives matter most. We mourn the loss of all of these lives and want to see an end to this violence across the United States, including in the iconic American city of New Orleans.

To achieve this, first, we need to ensure police accountability, prevent violent attacks on law enforcement, and improve the relationship between police officers and the communities that they are sworn to protect and serve. Community trust police—community trust policies are integral to smart law enforcement for diverse communities, including those with immigration populations like New Orleans and my district in Michigan.

Secondly, studies show that crime rates actually decrease after localities adopt community trust policies. Further, these studies find that strong-arm policies, such as Secure Communities, fail to lower crime rates. Instead, they make communities less safe because residents become more fearful and, therefore, less likely to report criminal activity or cooperate with investigations.

We share the common goal of community safety. To suggest that local leaders and law enforcement officials are purposefully pursuing policies that make their communities less safe is simply false and offensive.

Finally, if we are looking for real solutions, we should be undertaking comprehensive immigration reform. Unfortunately, this hearing, which pejoratively refers to New Orleans' community trust policy as a sanctuary city policy is not about comprehensive immigration reform. It is about anti-immigrant politics and fearmongering.

An immigration reform bill, such as the measure that passed the Senate in 2013 or the legislation that had 201 House cosponsors in the last Congress, would allow law-abiding immigrants to come out of the shadows and get right with the law, and it would enable immigration customs enforcement to focus its resources on deporting the worst elements. This kind of solution would help ensure that the city of New Orleans and all communities, citizens and immigrants alike, as well as the brave men and women serving in law enforcement are protected from harm.

And in closing, I thank the Chairman, and I look forward to a meaningful discussion in this hearing from our witnesses. Thank you, Mr. Chairman.

Mr. GOWDY. The gentleman from Michigan yields back.

We have a very distinguished panel of witnesses, and I will begin by swearing them in. If you would, please rise.

Do you swear the testimony you are about to give is the truth, the whole truth, and nothing but the truth, so help you God?

May the record reflect all the witnesses answered in the affirmative. You may sit down.

We will introduce you en banc, and then I will recognize you individually for your opening statements. First, it is my pleasure to welcome the Honorable Jeff Landry, who is the attorney general for the State of Louisiana. Attorney General Landry joined the Louisiana National Guard in high school, taking part in Operation Desert Storm, and served as both a police officer and a sheriff's deputy. General Landry ran successfully for Congress in 2010 and served in the 112th Congress. He became Louisiana's attorney general on January 11, 2016. He has a bachelor's of science degree from the University of Southwestern Louisiana, which is now the University of Louisiana at Lafayette, and a law degree from Loyola University New Orleans' law school.

Welcome, Attorney General Landry.

The Honorable Michael Horowitz is the inspector general for the Department of Justice. He worked as an assistant U.S. attorney for the Southern District of New York before joining DOJ in 1999 where he served as Deputy Assistant Attorney General and chief of staff in the Criminal Division of Main Justice from 1999 to 2002. General Horowitz also served as Commissioner of the U.S. Sentencing Commission. He was sworn into his current position on April 16, 2012. He graduated with highest honors from Brandeis University and earned his law degree with high honors from Harvard Law School.

Welcome, Inspector General Horowitz.

Next is my pleasure to introduce Ms. Vanita Gupta. She is the Principal Deputy Assistant Attorney General and the head of the Civil Rights Division at the Department of Justice. Ms. Gupta worked as a civil rights attorney and deputy director of the American Civil Liberties Union. She became head of the Civil Rights Division in 2014. She earned her undergraduate degree with high honors from the Yale University and a law degree from the New York University School of Law.

Welcome, Madam Attorney General.

And Mr. Zach Butterworth is the director of Federal Affairs for the city of New Orleans, representing Mayor Mitchell Landrieu in the New Orleans Police Department, the international airport, and the regional transit authority, and water infrastructure system. Mr. Butterworth served as the legislative director and counsel to Senator Mary Landrieu and as senior counsel to our friend, Congressman Cedric Richmond. Mr. Butterworth graduated from LSU and Loyola University New Orleans College of Law. Welcome to each of you.

Attorney General Landry, you are recognized for your 5-minute opening.

TESTIMONY OF THE HONORABLE JEFF LANDRY, ATTORNEY GENERAL, LOUISIANA DEPARTMENT OF JUSTICE

Mr. LANDRY. Thank you, Mr. Chairman, Madam Ranking Member, for the opportunity to address this Committee on one aspect of a public crisis of our time, and that is illegal immigration. As Louisiana's chief legal officer, I am committed to ensuring the rule of law is followed by everyone.

Like each of you, I took an oath to defend the Constitution, and I intend to uphold it. Unfortunately, sanctuary city policies undermine our justice system and our national security. As I am sure you agree, government's most important function is for providing and securing the safety of her citizens.

Sanctuary policies not only jeopardize the ability to protect our citizens, but they also allow illegals to commit crimes, then roam free in our communities. It has been reported that cities with sanctuary policies have seen an increase in crime. One sanctuary city, Los Angeles, saw all crimes rise in 2015. Violent crimes was up 20 percent; homicides up 10 percent; shootings victims up almost 13 percent; rapes up almost 9 percent; robberies up 12 percent; and aggravated assaults up 27 percent.

What is more, ICE recently reviewed that over 1,800 illegals released by sanctuary cities were later rearrested almost 4,300 times, committing almost 7,500 new crimes, including rape and child sex abuse.

Sanctuary policies encourage further illegal immigration and waste much-needed public resources as they force the Federal Government to find and arrest deportable criminals already taken into custody by local law enforcement.

This spring, I advocated for legislation in Louisiana that would have increased public safety by incentivizing the government—government agencies to follow the law. Because of this effort, Lafayette Parish is no longer a sanctuary city parish. As of late Friday, the city of New Orleans has changed its policy allowing NOPD to now allegedly cooperate with Federal authorities.

By shining a bright light on this dangerous procedure, this Committee has already provided a catalyst for change. Let me be clear: I am not trying to become the immigration police. Between catching child predators, rooting out public corruption, and fighting Federal overreach, I have more than enough to do. But I am here today to push for a change because the Administration has not only decided not to enforce the law, but they also have used their power to coerce local jurisdictions in my State to institute sanctuary city policies.

In the great city of New Orleans, the Justice Department entered into a consent decree with the city that mandated that its police officers not make inquiries into an individual's immigration status or assist ICE unless there is a warrant or court order issued.

As a former police officer and sheriff's deputy, I find it unconscionable that criminals who are in our country illegally cannot be held unless a—until a warrant or a court order is issued. After all, American citizens can be stopped on reasonable suspicion, arrested on probable cause, and may not see a judge for 2 to 3 days. Illegal immigrants should not be given a greater right than we afford our own citizens.

After hearing testimony in the statehouse in Louisiana that the Department of Justice, the U.S. Department of Justice, mandated that the city of New Orleans adopt a sanctuary city policy as part of the consent decree, I wrote a letter to Attorney General Loretta Lynch asking for clarification. The response that this Committee and I received was a lengthy non-answer that we have unfortunately come to expect from the Administration.

However, a recent report by the DOJ's own inspector general confirmed that sanctuary jurisdictions violate Federal law by prohibiting communication with ICE officials. Furthermore, it explicitly declared that local jurisdictions comply with all Federal laws in order to receive Federal grants. All the while, the Administration has been rewarding sanctuary cities with hundreds of millions of dollars of Federal tax money.

I was criticized by the Governor of Louisiana and the mayor for allegedly jeopardizing State funding with the legislation that I supported. The truth is that the U.S. DOJ's mandated policy upon the city is what is jeopardizing their funding. Besides fiscal and legal issues, there are homeland security issues. Due to sanctuary city policies, foreign terrorists, such as members of ICE, have the ability to travel to a sanctuary city, commit a minor offense, and remain protected from being identified. And in the current environment, why would we discourage cooperation between State and local law enforcement?

Reducing crime and saving lives are not a partisan issue. In fact, politics never came up when I met with the family of St. John the Baptist Parish fire chief, Spencer Chauvin's family. Chief Chauvin was killed last month in the greater New Orleans area by an illegal alien with a lengthy criminal background who was in our country. The questions were not Republican or Democrat, conservative or liberal. This grieving family simply asked one thing that this Committee, Congress, and the Administration should absolutely answer: Why do we have to wait for illegals to victimize our citizens in a violent manner before deporting them?

And I pose to you an even humbler one: Why cannot the State—why cannot State and Federal law enforcement work collaboratively to prevent these types of actions?

Honorable Members, we need sound immigration policy that begins with securing the border and enforcing the immigration laws already on the books. Congress must act to support those of us at the State and local level who have been fighting these reckless sanctuary city policies.

I am proud that our efforts exposing the actions of DOJ and the city of New Orleans have resulted in substantive changes with the city's policy. Because of the efforts we made in Louisiana, our State no longer has any jurisdictions prohibiting them from communicating with Federal immigration authorities. Today, Louisiana is safer because of these changes. Thank you very much, and I look forward to answering any of your questions.

[The prepared statement of Mr. Landry follows:]

Jeff Landry
Attorney General

State of Louisiana
DEPARTMENT OF JUSTICE
OFFICE OF THE ATTORNEY GENERAL
P.O. BOX 94005
BATON ROUGE
70804-9005

New Orleans: How the Crescent City became a Sanctuary City

Thank you, Mister Chairman and Madame Ranking Member, for the opportunity to address your committee on one aspect of the public safety crisis of our time: illegal immigration.

As Louisiana's chief legal officer, I committed to ensuring the rule of law is followed by everyone. Like each of you, I took an oath to defend the Constitution. This pledge shall not be broken.

Unfortunately, sanctuary policies undermine justice. They are flagrant disregards for the law we all took an oath to uphold and defend.

As I am sure you agree, government's most important function is providing safety and security to her people. Sanctuary policies not only jeopardize the ability to protect our people, but they also allow illegals to commit crimes then roam free in our communities.

It has been reported that cities with sanctuary policies have seen an increase in crime. One sanctuary city, Los Angeles, saw all crime rise in 2015: violent crime up 19.9%, homicides up 10.2%, shooting victims up 12.6%, rapes up 8.6%, robberies up 12.3%, and aggravated assault up 27.5%.

What is more: Immigration and Customs Enforcement recently revealed that 1,867 illegals released by sanctuary cities were later arrested 4,298 times with 7,491 new crimes – including rape and child sex abuse.

Sanctuary policies encourage further illegal immigration and promote an underground economy that sabotages the tax base.

Sanctuary policies also waste much-needed public resources as they force the federal government to find and arrest deportable criminals already taken into custody by local law enforcement.

This Spring, I advocated for legislation in Louisiana that would have increased public safety by incentivizing government to follow the law. A bill by Representative Valerie Hodges would give local officials the choice to cooperate with Immigration officials or to protect illegal aliens committing crimes and lose out on the ability to get state funds. A bill by Representative Jay Morris would create a private cause of action for the victims of these misguided policies.

Let me be clear: I am not trying to do the job of ICE or DHS. Between catching child predators, rooting out public corruption, and fighting federal overreach – I have more than enough to do to make Louisiana an even better place. But I am here today pushing for change because the Administration has not only decided to not enforce the law, but they have also used their power to coerce local jurisdictions in my State to institute sanctuary policies.

In my beloved New Orleans, the Justice Department entered into a consent decree with the City that mandated police officers not make inquiries into an individual's immigration status or assist ICE unless there is a warrant or court order issued.

As a former police officer and sheriff deputy, I find it unconscionable that criminals cannot be held on anything less than a warrant or a court order. After all – American citizens are detained on reasonable suspicion, arrested on probable cause, and may not see a judge for 2 to 3 days. Illegal immigrants should not be given greater rights than our own citizens have.

After hearing testimony in the Louisiana House that City of New Orleans deemed the DOJ consent decree as mandating their sanctuary policy, I wrote a letter to United States Attorney General Loretta Lynch asking for clarification. The response that this committee and I received was a lengthy, legally-worded non-answer that we have unfortunately come to expect from this Administration.

However, a recent report by DOJ's own Inspector General outlined the fact that sanctuary jurisdictions, like New Orleans, are in violation of federal law by prohibiting communication with ICE officials. Furthermore, it explicitly declared that local jurisdictions are required to be in compliance with all federal laws in order to receive federal grant dollars. All the while, the Administration has been rewarding sanctuary cities with hundreds of millions of dollars in federal grants.

Besides fiscal and legal issues, there are many health concerns. Additionally, there are homeland security issues. Foreign terrorists – such as members of ISIS – have the ability to travel to a city like New Orleans, commit a minor offense, and remain protected from being identified – due to sanctuary policies.

Reducing crime and saving lives are not partisan issues. In fact, politics never came up when I met with the family of St. John the Baptist Parish Fire Chief Spencer Chauvin. Chief Chauvin was killed last month in the Greater New Orleans Area by an illegal alien with a vast criminal background in our country.

The questions were not Republican or Democrat, conservative or liberal. Rather, this grieving family simply asked one thing that this Committee, Congress, and the Administration should absolutely answer: why do we have to wait for illegals to commit violent crimes before we can deport them?

And I pose to you an even humbler one: why is being in the United States illegally not a deportable offense?

Honorable Members, we need a sound immigration policy that begins with securing the border and enforcing the immigration laws already on the books. Congress must act to help support those of us at the State level who have been fighting sanctuary policies.

Thank you very much for your time, I look forward to answering your questions.

Mr. GOWDY. Thank you, Mr. Attorney General.
Inspector General Horowitz.

TESTIMONY OF THE HONORABLE MICHAEL E. HOROWITZ, INSPECTOR GENERAL, U.S. DEPARTMENT OF JUSTICE

Mr. HOROWITZ. Mr. Chairman, Ranking Members, Members of the Committee, thank you for inviting me to testify before you today.

Earlier this year, the Department advised the Office of Inspector General that it had received information indicating that jurisdictions receiving Department grant funds may be in violation of title 8 United States Code, section 1373. The Department provided the OIG with grant information related to more than 140 State and local jurisdictions and asked our office to review the allegations.

We considered the matter as requested and subsequently provided the Department with a memorandum advising it of the steps we had taken and summarizing the information we had learned. We did so expeditiously because, in part, the Department's grant process was ongoing, and we found that the Department had not provided grant recipients with clear guidance as to whether section 1373 was an applicable Federal law with which recipients were expected to comply in order to satisfy relevant grant rules and regulations.

Based on a large number of jurisdictions cited by the Department and the need for us to review this expeditiously, we judgmentally selected 10 State, and local jurisdictions for further review. For each jurisdiction, we researched the local laws and policies that govern their interactions with U.S. Immigrations and Customs enforcement and interviewed ICE officials to gain their perspective on ICE's relationship with the jurisdictions.

Based on our research, we found that the laws and policies of several jurisdictions went beyond placing limitations on complying with civil immigration detainer requests and potentially limited the sharing of immigration status information with Federal immigration authorities.

We also found that the laws and policies of some jurisdictions in our sample group that address the handling of ICE detainer requests might have had a broader practical impact on the level of cooperation with ICE and therefore might be inconsistent with the intent of section 1373. ICE officials expressed a similar concern to us.

With regard to the New Orleans Police Department, we noted that its then existing policy broadly prohibited officers from disclosing a person's citizenship and immigration status information with an exception where the disclosure was "required by Federal or State law."

This savings clause language appeared to be potentially inconsistent with the plain language of section 1373 because, for example, section 1373 doesn't "require" cooperation with ICE, but rather prevents jurisdictions from prohibiting or restricting employees from providing immigration status to ICE upon request.

In our memorandum, we advise the Department of several steps it could consider taking to the extent its focus was to ensure grant recipient compliance with section 1373. Among the steps were to provide clear guidance to grant recipients regarding whether they would be expected to comply with section 1373 in order to satisfy relevant grant rules and regulations, to require grant applicants to provide certifications and supporting documentation regarding compliance with section 1373, and to consult with the Department's law enforcement counterparts at ICE and other agencies regarding such issues prior to grant awards.

We believe the steps we outlined would provide the Department with assurances that a grant applicant was cooperating—was operating in compliance with section 1373 and also would be helpful should the Department later refer alleged violations of section 1373 by grant recipients to the OIG for our investigation.

This concludes my statement, and I will be pleased to answer any questions that the Committee may have.

[The prepared statement of Mr. Horowitz follows:]

Office of the Inspector General
United States Department of Justice

Statement of Michael E. Horowitz
Inspector General, U.S. Department of Justice

before the

U.S. House of Representatives
Committee on the Judiciary
Subcommittee on Immigration and Border Security

concerning

"New Orleans: How the Crescent City Became a Sanctuary City"

September 27, 2016

Mr. Chairman, Congresswoman Lofgren, and Members of the Subcommittee:

Thank you for inviting me to testify before you today. Earlier this year, the Department of Justice (Department or DOJ) Office of Justice Programs (OJP) advised the Office of the Inspector General (OIG) that it had received information indicating that several jurisdictions receiving Department grant funds may be in violation of 8 U.S.C. Section 1373 (Section 1373), and asked the OIG to investigate the allegations. Section 1373 provides that Federal, State, and local government officials cannot prohibit or restrict communication of information regarding the citizenship or immigration status of an individual to Federal immigration officials. Accompanying its request, the Department provided the OIG with grant-related information for more than 140 state and local jurisdictions that had active grant awards or received State Criminal Alien Assistance Program (SCAAP) payments in 2015. In addition, OJP provided a letter from Congressman John Culberson to the Attorney General regarding whether Department grant recipients were complying with Federal law, particularly Section 1373, and attached to this letter was a January 2016 study by the Center for Immigration Studies.

We reviewed the matter as requested by the Department and provided OJP with a memorandum advising it of the steps we had taken and summarizing the information we had learned. We did so expeditiously because, in part, the Department's grant process was ongoing and we found that the Department had not yet provided grant recipients with clear guidance as to whether Section 1373 was an "applicable federal law" that recipients were expected to comply with in order to satisfy relevant grant rules and regulations. The OIG memorandum can be found on our website at: https://oig.justice.gov/reports/2016/1607.pdf.

Summary of OIG Findings

Based on the large number of jurisdictions referred by OJP and the need to provide our review expeditiously, we judgmentally selected a sample of 10 state and local jurisdictions from the list provided to us by OJP for further review. For each of these jurisdictions, we researched the local laws and policies that govern their interactions with U.S. Immigration and Customs Enforcement (ICE), assessed these laws and policies, and interviewed ICE officials to gain their perspective on ICE's relationship with the selected jurisdictions.

While a primary and frequently-cited indicator of limitations placed on cooperation by state and local jurisdictions with ICE is how the particular jurisdiction handles immigration detainer requests, we noted that Section 1373 does not specifically address restrictions on cooperation with ICE detainer requests. We further noted that the Department of Homeland Security has made a legal determination that civil immigration detainers are voluntary in nature and that the ICE officials with whom we spoke told us that they are not enforceable against jurisdictions which do not comply.

Based on our research, we found that each of the 10 jurisdictions had laws or policies that placed limitations on how they could respond to an ICE detainer request. Some jurisdictions honored a detainer request when the subject had prior felony convictions, gang membership, or listing on a terrorist watchlist, while other jurisdictions did not honor a detainer request under any circumstances.

In addition, we found that the laws and policies of several of the jurisdictions we reviewed went beyond placing limitations on complying with civil immigration detainer requests and potentially limited the sharing of immigration status information with Federal immigration authorities. For example, one jurisdiction prohibited its employees from providing information about the citizenship or immigration status of any person "unless required to do so by legal process." This "savings clause" language appeared to us to be inconsistent with the plain language of Section 1373 because, for example, Section 1373 does not require cooperation with ICE through "legal process" but rather is intended to permit employees to provide immigration status information to ICE upon request. Moreover, to be effective, this "savings clause" provision presumably would have to render the restriction described in the ordinance null and void with respect to ICE requests for immigration status information, even though the very purpose of the ordinance was to restrict cooperation with ICE.

Similarly, we found that the laws and policies of other jurisdictions in our sample group that addressed the handling of ICE detainer requests might have a broader practical impact on the level of cooperation with ICE, and might be inconsistent with the intent of Section 1373. For example, one jurisdiction's prohibition relating to personnel expending their time responding to ICE inquiries could easily be read by employees and officers as prohibiting them from expending time responding to ICE requests relating to immigration status. While these policies do not explicitly restrict the sharing of information, they could cause local officials to apply them in a manner that prohibits or restricts cooperation with ICE, which would be inconsistent with Section 1373. Indeed, this concern was expressed to us by ICE officials.

Steps for the Department to Undertake

As we noted in our memorandum to the Department, in March 2016, OJP notified SCAAP and Edward Byrne Memorial Justice Assistance Grant (JAG) applicants about the requirement to comply with Section 1373, and advised them that if OJP received information that an applicant may be in violation of Section 1373, the applicant may be referred for further investigation to the OIG and may be subject to criminal and civil penalties, in addition to relevant OJP programmatic penalties.

In light of the Department's notification to grant applicants, we advised the Department that it should consider taking additional steps, including:

- Providing clear guidance to grant recipients regarding whether they would be expected to comply with Section 1373 in order to satisfy relevant grant rules and regulations;

- Requiring grant applicants to provide certifications specifying the applicants' compliance with Section 1373, along with documentation sufficient to support certification; and
- Ensuring grant recipients clearly communicate to their personnel the provisions of Section 1373, especially that employees cannot be prohibited or restricted from sending citizenship or immigration status information to ICE.

In addition, we suggested that the Department consult with ICE and other Federal agencies, prior to awarding a grant, to determine whether applicants are prohibiting or restricting the sharing of this information by employees with ICE.

We believe that these steps would provide the Department with assurances that the grant applicant was operating in compliance with Section 1373 and would also be helpful should the Department refer alleged violations of Section 1373 to the OIG for further investigation.

This concludes my prepared statement, and I will be pleased to answer any questions that the Subcommittee may have.

Mr. GOWDY. Thank you, Mr. Inspector General.
Madam Attorney General.

TESTIMONY OF THE HONORABLE VANITA GUPTA, PRINCIPAL DEPUTY ASSISTANT ATTORNEY GENERAL, CIVIL RIGHTS DIVISION, U.S. DEPARTMENT OF JUSTICE

Ms. GUPTA. Thank you. Good morning. Good morning, Chairman Goodlatte, Chairman Gowdy, Ranking Member Zoe Lofgren, and distinguished members of Subcommittee. Thank you for the opportunity to speak before you today about the Justice Department's work to advance public safety and promote effective, constitutional, and community-oriented policing.

Around the country, State and local law enforcement serve as the first line of defense for public safety. They keep our families safe from harm, they fight crime on our streets, and as recent events painfully remind us, they do this demanding, often dangerous work, at great sacrifice and great personal risk.

So let us make no mistake: the vast majority of men and women who wear the badge serve our communities with professionalism, with integrity, and with distinction. They deserve our deepest respect and our steadfast support. Yet when police departments engage in a pattern or practice of unconstitutional policing, their actions can severely erode community trust and profoundly undermine public safety.

In 1994, Congress charged the Justice Department with a responsibility to investigate law enforcement agencies for a pattern or practice of conduct that violates Federal law, and when necessary, to develop remedies to eliminate such misconduct.

Today, I will discuss our work with the New Orleans Police Department by explaining the problems we found and the reforms that the city agreed to implement. In May 2010, New Orleans Mayor Mitch Landrieu requested that the Justice Department conduct an independent investigation of NOPD's systems and operations. In a letter, Mayor Landrieu stated that he inherited a police force described by many as one of the worst police departments in the country.

Following our fact-driven and comprehensive investigation, we published our findings in a detailed 141-page letter. Among other violations, we found evidence that NOPD was unfairly enforcing the law or failing to enforce the law based on race, ethnicity, national origin, and other protected characteristics. These discriminatory policing practices eroded trust. Crime victims and witnesses, especially in Latino communities, felt afraid to share information with the police. This hurt public safety.

In the context of reporting crime, one community member told us, "Out of fear, we stay quiet." I know many law enforcement officials and leaders around the country understand these concerns and recognize the very critical and important link between community trust and public safety.

In 2012, New Orleans and the Justice Department entered into a comprehensive negotiated consent decree approved by the Federal court in 2013 to resolve our allegations of unlawful police misconduct. The decree requires NOPD to make important changes in policies and practices related to the use of force, stops, searches, and arrests, the prevention of discriminatory policing, and officer training oversight and supervision.

In February of this year, after seeking input from the New Orleans community, the court appointed monitor, the Federal district court, as well as the U.S. Departments of Justice and Homeland Security, NOPD issued a new policy to help officers provide services effectively and fairly to all people in the city, regardless of their immigration status or the color of their skin.

Last week, NOPD updated its policy to clarify that it complies with a specific Federal statute, 8 U.S.C., section 1373, to ensure that officers understand that they can send and receive information regarding an individual's immigration status and to most effectively advance nondiscriminatory policing. The policy also states that NOPD officers can take law enforcement action and assist in immigration enforcement when there is a threat to public safety, to execute criminal warrants, and to safely execute a court order.

By facilitating a culture of trust and cooperation, the policy will help local and Federal law enforcement protect public safety. The hardworking men and women of the New Orleans Police Department continue to do precisely that by fighting crime in partnering with Federal law enforcement to identify and prosecute people who have committed violent crimes.

We strongly believe that this policy will help restore trust with crime victims and witnesses, enhance the sharing of information, and, in so doing, make the entire New Orleans community safer. In New Orleans and in any city the Justice Department works with, real and lasting reform can't happen overnight, and we recognize the vital role of sustained collaboration with the entire community, from police officers to public officials and to community members.

And I want to commend officials from the city and the NOPD for their partnership throughout this process. And I view our dialogue today here as an important part of that same process about how police reform can help make the residents and officers of New Orleans safer for generations to come. I look forward to your questions.

[The prepared statement of Ms. Gupta follows:]

Department of Justice

STATEMENT OF

VANITA GUPTA
PRINCIPAL DEPUTY ASSISTANT ATTORNEY GENERAL
CIVIL RIGHTS DIVISION
U.S. DEPARTMENT OF JUSTICE

BEFORE THE

SUBCOMMITTEE ON IMMIGRATION AND BORDER SECURITY
COMMITTEE ON THE JUDICIARY
U.S. HOUSE OF REPRESENTATIVES

FOR A HEARING CONCERNING

NEW ORLEANS: HOW THE CRESCENT CITY BECAME A
SANCTUARY CITY

PRESENTED

SEPTEMBER 27, 2016

Good morning, Chairman [Trey] Gowdy, Ranking Member [Zoe] Lofgren, and distinguished members of the Subcommittee. Thank you for the opportunity to speak before you today about the Justice Department's work to advance public safety and promote effective, constitutional, and community-oriented policing. The Department of Justice works tirelessly to protect the civil rights and physical safety of all people in America. State and local law enforcement serve as the first line of defense for public safety. In communities around the country, police, sheriffs, and other law enforcement officers fight crime on our streets. They keep our families safe from harm. They save lives. And – as recent events painfully remind us – they do this demanding and often dangerous work at great personal risk and sacrifice. They deserve our deepest respect, our highest praise, and our steadfast support.

The Justice Department invests substantial resources and oversees a range of programs to support law enforcement agencies around the country. Through these efforts, we strive to advance constitutional policing, to protect officer and public safety, and to bolster trust in community-police relations. Our work spans an array of areas: providing funding and equipment, issuing guidance and technical assistance, conducting training, and leading enforcement actions. In New Orleans alone, the Department has awarded more than $11.3 million in local grants through its Office of Community Oriented Policing Services (COPS) to create or preserve positions for 80 officers since 2009.

New Orleans is also one of several cities adopting crime-fighting strategies as part of the Violence Reduction Network (VRN). The initiative is a comprehensive approach to reducing violent crime that complements the Attorney General's Smart on Crime Initiative and leverages existing Justice Department resources in communities around the country. A major focus area for New Orleans since it joined the VRN has been building its crime analysis capabilities to make better use of data in order to prevent, predict, and deter crime. In addition, in New Orleans and the greater New Orleans area, under the Bureau of Justice Assistance's VALOR Initiative, the VALOR Officer Safety and Wellness Program has trained approximately 261 law enforcement officers in officer safety, wellness, and resilience and approximately 87 law enforcement officers have received active shooter response training.

Let us make no mistake. The vast majority of men and women who wear the badge serve our communities with professionalism, with integrity, and with distinction. Yet when police departments engage in a pattern or practice of unconstitutional policing, their actions can severely erode community trust and profoundly undermine public safety. More than two decades ago, Congress recognized the connection between constitutional policing and public safety and charged the Justice Department with the responsibility of enforcing 42 U.S.C. § 14141, part of the Violent Crime Control and Law Enforcement Act of 1994. This statute authorizes us to investigate local law enforcement agencies for a pattern or practice of misconduct – such as excessive force or discriminatory policing – that violates federal law and, where necessary, to file litigation to ensure reform. A critical part of all § 14141 investigations is hearing directly from officers and community members. If we identify a pattern or practice of unlawful conduct, we try to negotiate a settlement agreement with the jurisdiction. These agreements typically are entered as court-approved consent decrees, overseen by an independent monitor to ensure lasting reform that serves the community's interests in public safety and equitable treatment.

While common themes tend to emerge during these investigations, we also know that each jurisdiction faces unique challenges and requires tailored remedies. Today, I'll discuss our work with NOPD by explaining the problems we found and the reforms the city agreed to implement. In May 2010, New Orleans Mayor Mitch Landrieu requested that the Justice Department conduct an independent investigation of NOPD's systems and operations. In a letter, Mayor Landrieu acknowledged that he "inherited a police force ... described by many as one of the worst police departments in the country," referencing "the number of violent crimes, incidents of rape, and malfeasance by members of the police department" and calling for a "complete transformation" of NOPD. During the next 10 months, we conducted a careful, fact-driven investigation. As we do in every investigation, we interviewed NOPD officers, supervisors, and command staff. We spoke with community members and government officials. We participated in more than 40 community meetings with advocates, civic leaders, and public officials. We reviewed a wide range of NOPD documents, policies, and data. And we observed police activity, including by participating in ride-alongs with officers and supervisors.

Following our investigation, in March 2011 we published our findings in a detailed 141-page letter. We found patterns of conduct by NOPD that violated the law and caused unnecessary harm to residents: excessive force and unconstitutional stops, searches, and arrests; biased policing, including racial and ethnic profiling; and a failure to effectively communicate with, and provide policing services to, residents with limited English proficiency (LEP). We found a failure to adequately investigate sexual assault and domestic violence. And we found that the police department failed officers themselves, providing inadequate training, supervision, and support. Taken together, these failures significantly undermined public safety.

Given the Subcommittee's interests, I want to focus my testimony specifically on the problems of discriminatory policing that we identified in New Orleans and the remedies that followed. People of many different races, ethnicities, and national origins live in New Orleans. African-American residents constitute roughly 60 percent of the city's population. Beginning in the mid-1970s, many Vietnamese immigrants began to settle in New Orleans. And in the years after Hurricane Katrina, New Orleans saw a significant number of Latino immigrants move to the city.

During our investigation, we found reasonable cause to believe that NOPD engaged in a pattern or practice of discriminatory policing. We found evidence that NOPD unfairly enforced the law – or failed to enforce the law – based on one's race, ethnicity, national origin, sex, sexual orientation, or gender identity. We found evidence that many officers engaged in biased policing by deciding whom to stop, search, or arrest based on a subject's race or ethnicity, rather than how she behaved or credible information that she engaged in criminal activity. And we found evidence that NOPD denied policing services to – or failed to take meaningful steps to communicate with – some communities because of biases or stereotypes. The discriminatory policing practices we documented broke the law. They also eroded trust between the police force and the city's residents. As a result, residents were less willing to share information with officers – information critical to solving and preventing crime – making the residents and the officers less safe.

Police officers cannot solve crimes – and therefore cannot help victims, prosecute criminals, or help federal law enforcement deport violent criminals – if victims and witnesses feel afraid to share information. In New Orleans, we heard from crime victims and community members who told us of the Latino community's strong belief that reporting crime may lead to unwanted attention or harassment from the police. Crime victims said that when they called the police for help, officers only asked about their immigration status, instead of addressing the physical safety threat they faced, or the other specific reason they called the police in the first place. Latino residents became afraid to encounter and interact with the police because they knew NOPD officers regularly stopped Latinos for minor offenses – behavior that would not ordinarily merit police activity – solely to question them about their immigration status. Interactions like these created fear and eroded trust. As one man testified in court at a fairness hearing about the problems facing day laborers, "these are the most common problems within our community: [t]hat my purse was stolen, they assaulted me, they robbed me, and we simply stay quiet, we don't call the police because we are afraid to call them, we don't trust them." As one community member told us: "Out of fear, we stay quiet." When communities fear the police, it undermines the officers' ability to fight crime and protect public safety.

Similarly, when police officers cannot effectively communicate with an entire group of community members, it undermines officers' ability to protect public safety and fight crime. In New Orleans, we found that the inability of NOPD officers to effectively communicate with LEP individuals – including Latino and Vietnamese immigrants – had harmful consequences. At the time of our investigation, NOPD relied primarily on just two officers – one fluent in Spanish and one fluent in Vietnamese – to assist on all service calls and investigations involving LEP residents. Testifying at a fairness hearing, one Spanish-speaking immigrant told the court about the problems caused by officers' inability to communicate with many residents: "[W]e don't feel safe, we don't feel supported. We, the immigrants don't feel support from them [the police]. We cannot call them for any kind of problem for help."

Law enforcement leaders around the country recognize the critical connection between community trust and crime prevention. As Tom Manger, Chief of Police for the Montgomery County, Maryland, Police Department and President of the Major Cities Chiefs Association (MCCA), said in his testimony before the Senate Judiciary Committee last year: "Whether we seek to stop child predators, drug dealers, rapists[,] or robbers – we need the full cooperation of victims and witness[es]." And he continued to explain the specific challenges facing immigrant communities: "When immigrants come to view their local police and sheriffs with distrust because they fear deportation, it creates conditions that encourage criminals to prey upon victims and witnesses alike." Other police chiefs and leaders of law enforcement professional associations have made similar comments, highlighting the importance of community trust to advance public safety.

In 2012, New Orleans and the Justice Department entered into a comprehensive consent decree – approved by the federal court in 2013 – to resolve our allegations of unlawful police misconduct. The decree requires NOPD to make important changes in policies and practices related to the use of force; stops, searches, and arrests; the prevention of discriminatory policing; and officer training, oversight, and supervision. The agreement requires NOPD to prioritize community interaction and partnerships, ensuring that its core operations support community policing. It requires NOPD and the city to develop and implement a comprehensive recruitment program to attract and hire a diverse group of qualified officers. And it requires NOPD to ensure that officers get access to mental health services, crisis counseling, and stress management training.

To prevent discriminatory policing, our consent decree requires NOPD to deliver policing services in an equitable, respectful, and bias-free manner. NOPD must ensure that all members of the public receive the equal protection of the law. To implement these changes, NOPD must effectively communicate with – as well as provide timely policing services to – all members of the community, regardless of their national origin or their ability to speak English. Accordingly, NOPD agreed to provide all officers with four hours of comprehensive training on bias-free policing.

In addition, to more effectively prevent and solve crimes, NOPD will provide all individuals in the city – regardless of immigration status – with essential police services. In practice, this means NOPD officers won't conduct investigations, make arrests, or take other law enforcement actions merely *because of* a subject's immigration status or the color of one's skin. This means officers won't question victims or witnesses about their immigration status unless for a legitimate law enforcement reason relevant to the investigation. NOPD officers can still take law enforcement action where individuals, whatever their immigration status, are wanted for a crime or where they have independent law enforcement reasons for doing so. For example, police can, of course, question or arrest someone suspected of committing a crime; assist with executing a criminal immigration warrant; share information and cooperate with federal authorities during criminal investigations, including in situations that might put officers and federal agents in danger; and enforce driving laws. NOPD agreed to widely distribute a written policy incorporating the requirements highlighted above. Clear and effective policies foster mutual trust and respect between officers and the residents they serve.

In February of this year – after seeking input from the New Orleans community, the court-appointed monitor, and the federal district court, as well as the U.S. Departments of Justice and Homeland Security – NOPD issued a new policy to help officers provide services effectively and fairly to all people in the city, regardless of their immigration status or the color of their skin. After this new policy was released, local officials and members of Congress raised concerns about NOPD's policy on immigration status, specifically regarding its compliance with a federal statute, 8 U.S.C. § 1373, which states that government entities and officials "may not prohibit, or in any way restrict, any government entity or official from sending to, or receiving from, the Immigration and Naturalization Service information regarding the citizenship or immigration status, lawful or unlawful, of any individual." In July, the Justice Department wrote to all recipients of the Edward Byrne Memorial Justice Assistance Grant (JAG) program and the State Criminal Alien Assistance Program (SCAAP), reaffirming that Section 1373 is an applicable federal law for the purposes of the JAG program and SCAAP. Following the issuance of the Department's guidance, the Civil Rights Division began working with New Orleans officials to update NOPD's policy on immigration status to clarify that the policy complies with Section 1373 and to most effectively advance non-discriminatory policing. Earlier this month, the parties and the independent monitor approved the revised language, and NOPD formally adopted it, clarifying that "[t]his policy is to be construed in accordance with 8 U.S.C. § 1373(a)."

The policy on immigration status (Chapter 41.6.1 in NOPD's Operations Manual) – along with several additional policies on the use of force, sexual assault, domestic violence, and crisis intervention, among other topics – provides officers with clear guidance to ensure non-discrimination in policing and to build trust between law enforcement and the entire New Orleans community. Of course, NOPD continues to investigate crimes and work with federal officials to arrest violent criminals regardless of their immigration status. This policy explicitly permits NOPD to assist victims and witnesses in obtaining U visas and T visas, where appropriate. These programs serve an important function in allowing victims and witnesses to help law enforcement prosecute violent crimes and human trafficking. By facilitating a culture of trust and cooperation – the new policy will help local and federal law enforcement advance, not impede, these critical goals of fighting crime, identifying and prosecuting people who have committed violent crimes, and protecting public safety. Under the decree, NOPD also agreed to annually review each new policy to ensure it provides clear direction to officers, remains consistent with the agreement, and complies with current law. And – as we do with every jurisdiction where we negotiate a consent decree – the Justice Department continues to work closely with NOPD, the city, the monitor, and the court as we engage in this rigorous review process for all policies.

As we engage on these issues, we must recognize the reality that thousands of immigrants and their families live in the city of New Orleans. Under our Constitution and laws, police must protect all people from violence and from harm. The hard-working men and women of the New Orleans Police Department continue to do precisely that by fighting crime and partnering with federal law enforcement to identify and prosecute people who have committed violent crimes. In New Orleans, and in any city the Justice Department works with, real and lasting reform can't happen overnight. We often get involved in communities precisely because systemic policy failures and constitutional violations – built up over decades – have created a culture of mistrust and disrespect. While we see promising signs of progress in New Orleans, we also know that real reform takes time. And we recognize the vital role of sustained collaboration and cooperation with the entire community: from public officials, to police officers, to community members. I want to commend Mayor Landrieu and NOPD Superintendent [Michael] Harrison for their partnership, their collaboration, and their cooperation throughout this process. And I view our dialogue today, with this Subcommittee, as an important part of that same process about how police reform can make the residents and officers of New Orleans safer for generations to come. Thank you, once again, for inviting me to speak with you today. I look forward to your questions.

Mr. GOWDY. Thank you, Madam Attorney General.

Mr. Butterworth.

TESTIMONY OF ZACH BUTTERWORTH, EXECUTIVE COUNSEL AND DIRECTOR OF FEDERAL AFFAIRS, OFFICE OF MAYOR MITCHELL J. LANDRIEU, CITY OF NEW ORLEANS

Mr. BUTTERWORTH. Chairman Gowdy, Chairman Goodlatte, Ranking Member Lofgren, and Congressmen, my name is Zach Butterworth. I am the executive counsel and director of Federal relations for the city of New Orleans. Thank you for giving me the opportunity to provide testimony before the Committee today.

Ms. GUPTA. Hold on. Now it is on.

Mr. BUTTERWORTH. Okay. Thank you, Vanita.

Ms. GUPTA. Sorry about that.

Mr. BUTTERWORTH. Before I begin, I would like to thank the panel for their support that Congress has provided to New Orleans since Hurricane Katrina 11 years ago. Our recovery would certainly not be where it is today without that support.

I would also like to thank you for your strong support of the victims of the flooding of Baton Rouge. I have seen a magnitude of that flood, and those people will certainly need your help for years to come.

I want to emphasize three main points from my written testimony and then try to give the panel a little bit of context for how we got here today. First, public safety is a top priority in New Orleans. Legal or undocumented, whoever commits a crime in New Orleans will be arrested. Our record shows that every day the New Orleans Police Department takes violent criminals off the streets.

In 2012, Mayor Landrieu formed the Multi-Agency Gang Unit. That unit alone has arrested 100 of the most violent criminals in New Orleans. Murder is down in New Orleans, 18 percent from 2011. At the same time, murder was up 4 percent nationwide. Violent crime is down in New Orleans, 60 percent dating back to its highs in 1994.

My second point is that New Orleans' policy does not make us a sanctuary city. We are trying to follow Federal law. We have been trying to follow Federal law from day 1. It should go without saying that any police department—any policy a police department adopts follows State, local, and Federal law.

So the review process here. The NOPD, every policy is reviewed by the Department of Justice, a Federal monitor, who is appointed by a Federal judge, and the NOPD.

In drafting our policy, we asked the experts. Officials from ICE were brought in and reviewed best practices from around the country. For instance, the Major Cities Chiefs Association, which New Orleans is a member, represents 70 million Americans. They support policies that foster trust, cooperation between police officers, and immigrant communities that we all serve.

And my third point is that NOPD's policy on immigration status will make the city safer. It frees up our officers to focus on violent crime. It also allows anyone to report a crime or to be a witness or a victim to report a crime. The policy is already bearing fruit. On the ground, our commanders are seeing better cooperation with immigrant communities.

Quickly, going back to 2010, we did invite the Justice Department in. Their comprehensive investigation showed that we had problems in the way that we treated the immigrant community. We wanted to fix that.

Since 2010, we have launched 11 new recruit classes. We have written 34 of these types of policies. Forty more are being drafted right now. These policies cover canine use, prisoner transport, Taser operations, body-worn cameras, to name a few.

Now, going back to March 2015, we started drafting this policy with the NOPD, the Federal monitor, and of course, the Justice Department. In September, we brought in ICE. We asked the experts. They were brought in at both the local and the headquarters level. At the time, ICE told us that the policy complied with all Federal ICE requirements for law enforcement.

Then in December, Judge Susie Morgan, who oversees the consent decree, also brought in ICE. We had the chief counsel from the New Orleans division in our office. No concerns, substantive concerns, about the policy were raised at that time.

So, in February of this year, the Federal monitor approved the policy. Immediately, there were some concerns about the policy, so Mayor Landrieu wrote to DHS and DOJ, the leadership there, and said: "If anyone in any of your agencies, any person has a concern about this policy, please contact us." It wasn't until July that we received a letter back with information about 1373 and general compliance there.

So, when we got that—when we received that information, we immediately went to work redrafting the policy with DOJ, and as the Chairman noted, last week, the Federal monitor did approve the updated policy that we believe fully complies with Federal law just as we believe the last policy fully complied with Federal law.

So, simply put, the NOPD's policy on immigration status is going to make the city safer, and it follows Federal law. As required by the consent decree, we will review our policies continuously, and I am happy to take any questions. Thank you.

[The prepared statement of Mr. Butterworth follows:]

TESTIMONY OF

ZACH BUTTERWORTH

ON BEHALF OF THE

CITY OF NEW ORLEANS

AND

NEW ORLEANS POLICE DEPARTMENT

BEFORE THE

JUDICIARY COMMITTEE

SUBCOMMITTEE ON IMMIGRATION AND BORDER SECURITY

CHAIRMAN GOWDY, PRESIDING

UNITED STATES HOUSE OF REPRESENTATIVES

HEARING:

New Orleans: How the Crescent City Became a Sanctuary City

September 27, 2016 10:00 AM

Chairman Gowdy, Ranking Member Lofgren and members of the committee: I am Zach Butterworth, Executive Counsel and the Director of Federal Relations for the City of New Orleans. Thank you for inviting me to provide testimony to the Committee as it considers these important issues.

Before I delve into my testimony, I want to emphasize three points:

1.   Public safety is our top priority in New Orleans. Anyone — legal or undocumented — who commits a violent crime in New Orleans will be arrested. Our record shows that every day, the New Orleans Police Department (NOPD) works closely with federal and state law enforcement agencies to keep violent criminals off our streets. In 2012, Mayor Landrieu formed the Multi-Agency Gang (MAG) Unit to bring the most violent criminals to justice. The MAG Unit consists of law enforcement officials from NOPD, Orleans Parish District Attorney's Office, Orleans Parish Sheriff's Office, Louisiana State Police, Parole Board of the Louisiana Department of Corrections, United States Attorney's Office, Federal Bureau of Investigation, Bureau of Alcohol, Tobacco, Firearms, and Explosives, Drug Enforcement Administration, United States Marshal's Service, and the United States Probation & Parole Office for the Eastern District of Louisiana. To date, prosecutions by the MAG Unit have led to the conviction of more than 100 violent criminals.

2.   The NOPD's policy does not make New Orleans a sanctuary city — we are following federal law.

3.   The NOPD's policy on immigration status will make our city safer by allowing officers to focus on protecting the public and ensuring that everyone is able to report crimes and cooperate as witnesses. The policy is bearing fruit. In the last few months, a hispanic male was approached

by an armed individual who placed the gun to his head and robbed him. The victim called the police and the assailant was apprehended. This victim cooperated with the DA's office as well as NOPD and another violent criminal is off the streets — convicted of armed robbery.

For generations, New Orleans, like many communities, has seen tension between the police and the community. When Mayor Landrieu took office in 2010, the U.S. Department of Justice (DOJ) had already launched a series of investigations related to civil rights abuses by officers in the Department. It was clear that changes were needed, so Mayor Landrieu immediately requested that the DOJ step in to help reform the Department.[1] At the time, the public rightly demanded that the police operate in a manner consistent with the Constitution and all federal, state and local laws.

In 2012, the NOPD and the DOJ entered into a comprehensive Consent Decree that reflected years of work and a shared commitment to effective, constitutional and professional law enforcement. The Consent Decree contains an array of separate requirements detailed in more than 492 paragraphs and 122 pages.

Since then, we have completely overhauled the NOPD. We have launched 11 new recruit classes and put in place 34 new operational policies that continue to transform the culture of the Department. The new policies cover use of force, K9 use, proper prisoner transport, taser operation, body-worn camera operation and how officers should respond to reports of sexual assault, to name just a few.

---

[1] New Orleans has a unique political structure. The mayor and sheriff represent separate and distinct political subdivisions that are independently elected by the citizens of New Orleans. The mayor is elected parish-wide to lead the executive branch of government, including the NOPD. The Orleans Parish Sheriff is elected parish-wide to oversee the jail, which is currently under the operational control of a federally appointed compliance director.

To ensure constitutionality, workability and consistency, every policy that the NOPD adopts is approved by the Federal Consent Decree Monitor[2] (Federal Monitor) and the DOJ's Civil Rights Division. It should go without saying that all policies must promote public safety and adhere to local, state and federal laws. Additionally, the entire Consent Decree falls under the oversight of Judge Susie Morgan of the United States District Court for the Eastern District of Louisiana.

This same process was followed in the drafting of the original and revised policies, Chapter 41.6.1, Immigration Status. Additionally, we engaged officials from the Department of Homeland Security (DHS) Immigration and Customs Enforcement (ICE) and reviewed best practices around the country. For instance, the Major City Chiefs Association, which represents law enforcement agencies covering 70 million Americans, supports policies that foster trust and cooperation between police officers and immigrant communities.

Beginning in September 2015, the City and NOPD held multiple discussions with ICE, both local and headquarters, to determine the requirements for local police departments regarding the treatment of undocumented immigrants. At that time, ICE verbally told NOPD that the draft policy complied with all ICE requirements.

Further, on December 1, 2015, Judge Morgan called a meeting with NOPD, ICE, DOJ and the Federal Monitor to give ICE agents the opportunity to raise any concerns with the new policy. Five ICE agents attended the meeting including the Chief Legal Counsel in the New Orleans field office. The local ICE representatives did not raise any substantive issues in the meeting, and were told to contact the monitor with any further concerns with the policy.

---

[2] In 2013. U.S. District Judge Susie Morgan selected the law firm of Sheppard, Mullin, Richter and Hampton as the Federal Consent Decree Monitor.

After the policy was thoroughly reviewed by the Federal Monitor, DOJ and NOPD, Federal Monitor David Douglass approved it on February 2, 2016. Mr. Douglass noted in the approval letter that the new policy "sets forth clear and appropriate rules to guide officer conduct."

On March 3, 2016, Mayor Landrieu wrote to Attorney General Loretta Lynch and Department of Homeland Security Secretary Jeh Johnson, requesting that they contact the Federal Monitor if any officials within DHS or DOJ had concerns that the policy did not fully comply with any federal law. On July 7, 2016, the DOJ, on behalf of both agencies, responded with general guidance regarding 8 U.S.C. § 1373.

After receiving the guidance from DOJ, the NOPD's compliance bureau reengaged the DOJ Civil Rights Division and the Federal Monitor. Out of an abundance of caution, we discussed changes to the policy that would ensure clarity regarding 8 U.S.C. §1373.

On September 22, 2016, the Federal Monitor, working with DOJ's Civil Rights Division, and the NOPD, approved modifications to the NOPD's policy. In approving the policy, the Federal Monitor stated that "[o]ur approval is also based on the representation by the Department of Justice that this policy complies with 8 U.S.C. §1373."

The NOPD's policy on immigrant status follows federal law and will make New Orleans safer. As required by the Consent Decree, the NOPD will annually review all policies to ensure that they prioritize public safety, best practices and current law.

Mr. GOWDY. Thank you, Mr. Butterworth.

The Chair will now recognize the gentleman from Virginia for his 5 minutes of questioning.

Mr. GOODLATTE. Well, thank you, Mr. Chairman.

Mr. Butterworth, let me pick right up where you left off. I appreciate the work that you have done on this, but under the revised policy, the New Orleans Police Department officers are prohibited from making inquiries about an individual's immigration status, including to ICE, yet section 1373(b) authorizes officers to make requests to ICE for such information.

So doesn't the policy violate Federal law, section 1373(b)?

Mr. BUTTERWORTH. Sir, we believe the policy fully complies with 1373. If there is anything about the new policy that is unclear, we would be happy to go back and take a look.

Mr. GOODLATTE. Why was there a specific reference made to 1373(a) and 1373(b) was left out of the——

Mr. BUTTERWORTH. I think the focus of the concerns that had been raised had been on 1373(a). I think, on behalf of the NOPD, we are happy to go back and make sure that there is no misunderstanding about 1373(b). I think, as you just heard, Ms.——

Mr. GOODLATTE. Are you aware of any concerns on the part of the mayor or city officials or the police department chief or others about authorizing officers to make inquiries about an individual's immigration status?

Mr. BUTTERWORTH. So, as you just heard Ms. Gupta testify, this policy allows officers to communicate with ICE. They are going to help ICE in any sort of public safety event. They are going to help ICE execute criminal warrants. And there is no restriction on the communication between an officer and ICE in this policy.

Mr. GOODLATTE. Is there any restriction on a police officer making a request to ICE for information regarding an individual's immigration status?

Mr. BUTTERWORTH. There is no—so the way the policy is laid out, if a person—if an officer interacts with a member of the public, he or she immediately run that person's name against the NCIC database system. If there is a return that there is a criminal warrant on that person, the person is immediately arrested.

Mr. GOODLATTE. And now you noted in your testimony that the New Orleans Police Department takes criminals off the street. If you find that they are not lawfully present in the United States, what happens after they have been through the judicial process in New Orleans?

Mr. BUTTERWORTH. So thank you for allowing me to clarify that. New Orleans has a very unique political structure. The mayor is elected parishwide, our counties, to lead the NOPD. Our sheriff is also elected parishwide, and he leads the sheriff's department. So I don't represent the sheriff's department, and I apologize that I can't speak on behalf of them, but our officers, who arrest someone on a criminal warrant, deliver the suspect——

Mr. GOODLATTE. So, assuming that they are prosecuted and convicted and incarcerated, not all will be, but those who are, after they have served their time, what does the policy of the New Orleans Police Department and courts say about communications with ICE about the fact that someone is about to be released from jail or released from prison who has been convicted of a crime and is not lawfully present in the United States?

Mr. BUTTERWORTH. So, if a person is convicted of a felony in Louisiana, they are likely sent to Angola, which is a State corrections facility, and I would defer to the attorney general on the operations of the State corrections facility after that.

Mr. GOODLATTE. And what about the New Orleans jails?

Mr. BUTTERWORTH. Again, the sheriff of New Orleans operates the jail there, and we have no operational control over the sheriff.

Mr. GOODLATTE. Thank you.

Well, let me turn to the attorney general. Welcome. We are glad to have you back with us, Attorney General Landry, and I want to start by asking you if you believe, as Louisiana's chief law enforcement officer, that the New Orleans consent decree violates Federal law.

Mr. LANDRY. I believe that, prior to the substantive changes that they made, it absolutely violated Federal law. The question is whether or not in practice the new changes will remedy that situation.

You know, what we have in the country is basically two types of sanctuary city policies. It is either a "don't ask" policy or "don't tell." What the current New Orleans city—what the prior policy was, prior to the change, was both, both a "don't ask" and "don't tell." Now the question is whether or not they—they seem to have remedied the "don't tell" portion of that policy, but it doesn't seem that they have made any changes in the "don't ask" portion.

Mr. GOODLATTE. And it is your intention to make sure that everything within your power to assure that that happens will happen so that they are in full compliance with 1373, not just one subsection of it.

Mr. LANDRY. Absolutely. We are going to try to take it upon ourselves to go out and let all law enforcement officers around the State know exactly what 1373 states and how they can avoid violating that statute.

Mr. GOODLATTE. Thank you. And just, in general, do you believe it is inconsistent for a jurisdiction to adopt a sanctuary policy that violates Federal law and at the same time requests Federal law enforcement grant money?

Mr. LANDRY. I do.

Mr. GOODLATTE. And what message does that send concerning the rule of law?

Mr. LANDRY. Well, again, it sends a terrible one. I think that is part of the demise of our criminal justice system and the reason that we have an uptick in crime across the country. When we allow people to flagrantly violate any law and then we just turn a blind eye to it, all that does is lead to those people committing additional crimes and thinking it is okay to break the law.

Mr. GOODLATTE. Well, thank you very much. And I heard your testimony that, with the correction of this, when hopefully it will soon be completely corrected, there will be no communities in the State of Louisiana that would be characterized as sanctuary cities.

Mr. LANDRY. Thank you, Mr. Chairman.

Mr. GOODLATTE. Well, thank you. I wish other States had the same effort to have such a consistent record.

And I yield back to the Chairman.

Mr. GOWDY. The gentleman from Virginia yields back. The Chair will now recognize the gentlelady from California, Ms. Lofgren.

Ms. LOFGREN. Thank you, Mr. Chairman.

Ms. Gupta, I understand that in 2005, the civil rights division was involved in investigating New Orleans policy abuse and misconduct in the aftermath of Hurricane Katrina. Can you talk briefly about the acts of abuse your division uncovered as a result of that investigation?

Ms. GUPTA. So we launched our investigation into the New Orleans Police Department in 2010 and uncovered very pervasive, widespread acts of misconduct related to specifically excessive use of force, stop searches, and arrests; discriminatory policing, and the like.

And one of the goals that we had when we had come in at the invitation of Mayor Landrieu was to ensure that the New Orleans Police Department would be able to carry out its core function of providing effective policing and constitutional policing to keep all residents of New Orleans safe. And in our 141-page findings report, we detailed, after extensive data, interviews, a lot of engagement with NOPD officers and command staff as well as community members that these violations had thoroughly undermined the NOPD's ability to solve and prevent crime in New Orleans. And in the years since, since we have enacted this consent decree, we have been working collaboratively with the city and with the brave men and women of the New Orleans Police Department to address these and to finally give New Orleans police officers the tools that they need to have the trust of all of their residents and to be able to fight violent crime.

Ms. LOFGREN. Thank you.

We are pleased to be joined today by a Member of the full Judiciary Committee, who is not a Member of the Subcommittee, and that is Mr. Richmond, who also represents New Orleans, and so I would like to yield the remainder of my time to him so that he might ask a question since this is his territory.

Mr. GOWDY. The gentleman from Louisiana is recognized.

Mr. RICHMOND. Thank you, Mr. Chairman, and thank you to the Ranking Member for allowing me to ask some questions.

Let me just start with a couple of things here. And in the opening testimony of our Chairman, he said that he believed that the consent decree between the City of New Orleans and the Department of Justice was done through collusion. And I will just tell you that as an African-American male who grew up in New Orleans who had to deal with the New Orleans Police Department, the police department went under consent decree because of use of force, failing to investigate it, stop and searches without cause, discrimination against African-Americans, failing to investigate sex crimes against females in domestic violence, a paid detail system that invited corruption, failing to sufficiently embrace community policing, and immigration as one of them. So I just would like to clear up for anyone who thinks that, you know, we colluded all of that, it is very convenient for a White male from Virginia to talk about collusion in a consent decree.

And Attorney General Landry, let me just applaud you for working on sanctuary cities, because you believe it is important, but I would ask, can you help our Chairman Goodlatte, because he has two sanctuary cities in Virginia, and if you are going to start cleaning up, start cleaning up at home. And while we go down the list, we have four in South Carolina, every parish in Colorado, we have Sioux City in Representative King's district, we have Rockwall, Dallas, and Travis in Texas. So if we are going to start talking about sanctuary cities, don't just pick mine that you would like to allege is a sanctuary city; let's talk about all of them, especially the people who are on the Committee.

And the other thing that we talked about was the unfortunate death of a fire chief, a very respected and loved fire chief in St. John Parish. And I think that incident happened because the person fell through the cracks, and that is what we should stop, but that has absolutely nothing to do with New Orleans. The guy didn't live in New Orleans, he was never arrested in New Orleans, the company he worked for was not in New Orleans. That has absolutely no connection to the city of New Orleans. Now, the company was operated out of St. Tammany Parish with an elected official as a co-owner, which I think is deplorable, and I think that that we should be looking at prosecution for, the owners of the company, but to just single out New Orleans as some city that decided all of a sudden that we wouldn't enforce the law is just incorrect.

Zach, Mr. Butterworth, let me just ask you a question. When did you all initiate trying to make sure that the city's policy was consistent with Federal law?

Mr. BUTTERWORTH. So we began drafting this policy in March of 2015 and we began discussions with ICE in September. So those have continued on both the local and headquarters level, and at no point did anyone at ICE ever say that this policy didn't comply with Federal law.

Mr. RICHMOND. And Ms. Gupta, at what point is it your office's opinion that they did not comply with Federal law? If at any time, did they not comply with Federal law?

Ms. GUPTA. The Justice Department believes the policy, even in February, complied with Federal law, the revisions that we just put into effect were made out of an abundance of caution after we received inquiries from officials in Louisiana as well as we reviewed our inspector general's memo, and in an abundance of caution, to ensure total clarity about the fact that the policy must comply with 1373, we literally lifted the language of the statute, put it into the policy to make it very clear that NOPD officers can share information with ICE regarding an immigration status or citizenship status of an individual, they can assist in operations in response to direct threats to public safety or where there is an independent law enforcement reason for doing so, they can assist in executing a criminal warrant, they can assist in the enforcement of court orders. So the revision was made to ensure total clarity with compliance with Federal law.

Mr. RICHMOND. So in summary, the old policy and the new policy, it is your opinion both were consistent with Federal law?

Ms. GUPTA. Yes.

Mr. RICHMOND. And, Mr. Horowitz, do you have an opinion on that?

Mr. HOROWITZ. We ultimately, Congressman, didn't reach a final determination as to the legality or not of the issue, primarily because of the fact that we needed to get the report back to the Department and its request expeditiously. And in order to do that, we would really need to be on the ground, go to the city, look at some of the issues that have been previously—had previously been raised, talk with folks on the ground there both from the city and from ICE, and we haven't taken those steps and I am not in a position to give a legal determination at this point without taking a full effort in that regard.

Mr. RICHMOND. Thank you. And I will yield back.

Mr. GOWDY. The gentleman from Louisiana yields back. The Chair will now recognize the gentleman from Idaho, Mr. Labrador.

Mr. LABRADOR. Thank you, Mr. Chairman. Sanctuary city policies have transformed some of our greatest American cities. I am increasingly frustrated by these policies that are consistently implemented in the name of ''unbiased and community-based'' policing, as Deputy Attorney General Gupta has said.

The ramifications for public safety and the inability for ICE to complete its mission are severe, and not only affect the cities, but the surrounding communities are impacted as well. While some of the witnesses today, including Deputy Attorney General Gupta, would like to ignore this fact, the simple truth is that immigration enforcement is a critical function of the United States Government and one that must be supported and not undermined in this form.

Much of this debate centers around the practical application of 8 USC 1373 and whether a city that has implemented sanctuary policies can simultaneously comply with this section of law.

Mr. Horowitz, based on your findings, what do you believe that 8 USC 1373 requires of local jurisdictions?

Mr. HOROWITZ. In Sections 1373(a) and 1373(b), I will combine them for purposes of just mentioning this, it essentially prohibits State, local, or Federal law from prohibiting or restricting in any way employees of those entities from sending to, requesting from, or receiving from ICE, information about the immigration status of an individual.

Mr. LABRADOR. So what do you make of the fact that Mr. Butterworth keeps saying that it complies, but nothing in their guidance says that they have the ability to request information?

Mr. HOROWITZ. The new policy that we also received on Friday afternoon and have looked at doesn't reference the word ''requesting,'' which is in (b)(1) of 1373.

Mr. LABRADOR. So it clearly doesn't fully comply. It seems to comply with (a), but not with (b).

Mr. HOROWITZ. It clearly addresses (a)——

Mr. LABRADOR, It clearly addresses (a).

Mr. HOROWITZ [continuing]. It doesn't include the word ''requesting,'' which is in (b). Again, without us understanding more, I am not going to be in a position to make a legal opinion on whether it complies——

Mr. LABRADOR. But it is a simple word.

Mr. HOROWITZ [continuing]. Or doesn't, but it omits the word "request."

Mr. LABRADOR. The missed "request"—the word "request" is not in the policy, correct?

Mr. HOROWITZ. That is correct.

Mr. LABRADOR. Okay. And you believe that we may need to clarify this section, correct?

Mr. HOROWITZ. I think it is an open question. I have gotten it— I got it Friday afternoon as well. I would have to do follow up, but with the absence of the word "requesting," which is in 1373(b) is obviously a reasonable question here.

Mr. LABRADOR. Okay. Attorney General Landry, great to have you here. Thank you so much for the work that you are doing. Do you believe that by implementing these sanctuary policies, New Orleans, and in particular NOPD, are promoting public safety?

Mr. LANDRY. Implementing the policies of sanctuary——

Mr. LABRADOR. Yeah.

Mr. LANDRY. Absolutely not. I mean, it is a danger to public safety. And what happens is it actually—you know, when you have— most of these cities are very large cities and you have a very large metropolitan footprint. What happens is it draws, it creates a magnet, a draw for illegal aliens as a sanctuary area for them to operate. It also creates an opportunity for—if you are a member of the drug cartel in Mexico, where would you send those people who are plying your illegal trade? You would send them into those cities, because the ability for those members to be identified is reduced because of the sanctuary city policies.

Mr. LABRADOR. Is New Orleans a safer city today than before implementing these sanctuary policies?

Mr. LANDRY. Well, certainly the substantive changes that they made on Friday is a step in the right direction. I think that going ahead and clarifying it and then actually determining whether or not there will be a collaborative effort to crack down on illegal immigration, especially those that are in custody that NOPD has arrested and identifies them, is yet to be seen.

Mr. LABRADOR. So as a law enforcement official, as someone who has served at both the Federal and State level, what do you believe is the appropriate relationship between local or State law enforcement and Federal immigration enforcement?

Mr. LANDRY. I believe they have to have extreme collaboration. I believe that, you know, based upon some of the U.S. Supreme Court's holding, that Congress needs to clarify exactly how law enforcement agents may engage in those types of questioning. And then, of course, implementing 1373 is certainly a step in the right direction, making sure that law enforcement agents know that they can ask and they can communicate with ICE in order to get those violent criminals off the street and deportable.

Mr. LABRADOR. Thank you. I yield back my time.

Mr. GOWDY. The gentleman from Idaho yields back. The Chair would now recognize the gentleman from Illinois, Mr. Gutierrez.

Mr. GUTIERREZ. Thank you. I would like to note that we are not having a hearing today about gun violence, 500 people shot dead in Chicago, 3,000 this year; we are not having a hearing about police killing unarmed civilians; we are not having a hearing about the need for immigration reform or detention centers; we are not having a hearing about any of the really important things. We are having a hearing about a Donald Trump talking point that one he goes to again and again, the one he says that immigrants are killers, rapists, drug dealers, who are here to hurt people, not to build up our country like every other immigrant group that has come before them.

Today we are focusing on one of America's great cities, a city with a troubling past when it comes to respecting civil rights and building trust between the police and the community at large. And so I would think that we would want to work on building that trust between the police and the people, and that the efforts taken by people to build that trust shouldn't be undermined.

Lastly, I am just going to say, because it doesn't really matter, this hearing, it really doesn't. It is going to come and go. You guys got somebody to pay for your trips to come down here. It is not going to have an impact on anything. We are not going to change anything. This is just another political hearing.

But I just want to say that, you know, we could have actually spoken to a lot of very important issues that people want us to talk about, but it always seems the majority always says we should listen to people that are not in Washington, D.C., we should listen to local elected officials, that that is where democracy is blooming, but it seems like every time you guys say anything, they have an objection when they don't like it.

So having said that, I just want to say to my colleague from New Orleans, I would like to yield the remaining 3 minutes of my time to Mr. Richmond to ask questions.

Mr. RICHMOND. Thank you.

Attorney General Landry, you said that New Orleans' policy would invite undocumented immigrants because of its status as a sanctuary city. New Orleans' foreign born population is about 6 percent. Neighboring Jefferson Parish, which is not a sanctuary city, is about 11 percent. How do we reconcile that with the notion that New Orleans is becoming a safe haven for undocumented people?

Mr. LANDRY. Let me clarify that. That was a misunderstanding, Congressman Richmond. The metropolitan area becomes—as a whole, invites illegal immigrants into that particular area, because, again, they feel the need, the ability to travel freely. Again, when you look at not only the actual city that implements the policies, it affects the surrounding areas.

Just last weekend in the Lafayette metropolitan area, we had an elderly man get hit head-on by an illegal immigrant, who, again, had been arrested multiple times and yet was not deportable. So here we have another family losing another loved one in an area which had—previously had a sanctuary city policy.

Mr. RICHMOND. And, look, I don't—you know, we have a great working relationship, and I know you are very tough on crime. Let me ask about the incident that killed our fire chief. The company was owned by a person in Louisiana and a State rep from Arkansas. Under Louisiana law, do you have the ability to indict the owners of the company for hiring an undocumented without a license that was driving when he caused that fatal accident?

Mr. LANDRY. In Louisiana, I believe the employment of an illegal is not a criminal offense, it is a civil matter.

Mr. RICHMOND. Well, if it is done in a very negligent manner and without—gross negligence, I think we do have some criminal statutes under which—let me just ask this, then. If we can find some criminal statutes under which to charge the owners of the company, who ultimately are at fault for hiring an undocumented, would you commit to charging them if the facts fit the statute? And I don't mind looking myself.

Mr. LANDRY. Yeah, absolutely. You know, Congressman, you are right, we have a great working relationship and I certainly respect you. And, yes, I intend to uphold the rule of law regardless.

You know, I would also mention that the sanctuary city legislation that we put forth in the State house just this year passed the State house with large bipartisan support. I think everyone is recognizing that this is a public safety debacle and that this is a first step in ensuring that our communities are safe.

Mr. RICHMOND. Thank you. And I would yield back.

Mr. GOWDY. The gentleman from Louisiana yields back. The Chair would now recognize the gentleman from Iowa, Mr. King.

Mr. KING. Thank you, Mr. Chairman. I thank the witnesses for your testimony here today. And I would turn first to Attorney General Landry, and I would like to—I would like to pose a broader concept here and then ask you to comment on that, and perhaps we will go a little deeper, and that is that, as I read Federal law and immigration law and as I understand it after these years on this Committee, it envisions in its entirety essentially vacuuming up the illegal people in the United States and all of those whom are encountered by law enforcement, it anticipates their removal from the United States, and it requires that when at least Federal law enforcement officers encounter someone who is unlawfully present in America, that they shall place them in removal proceedings.

Would you agree so far with my characterization of Federal law?

Mr. LANDRY. I do. I agree with that.

Mr. KING. And then, so when I look at this, this statute, 1373, and I read through the details of 1373, shouldn't it be clear to anyone who intends to comply with the intent of Federal law that they are to help facilitate rather than frustrate the intent of Federal law?

Mr. LANDRY. I agree. You know, just placing the type of language that has been put in the consent decree dealing with immigration frustrates the law.

Mr. KING. And I happen to have a little quote here from Mr. Richmond in a markup March 18, 2015, which was about the time of the inception of this situation. He is concerned about the police department and the sheriff's office, who have a Federal consent decree, and that they can comply with—this is a quote, "They are complying with a Federal consent decree, and now it will cause the City of New Orleans to lose valuable Federal money in terms of DHS and FEMA funds." I think it has been known that there has been a clear violation here of at least the intent of the consent decree—or excuse me, the intent of 1373 by the consent decree and the underlying policy, which is a sanctuary city policy, by my reading of it.

Have you had any discussions or have you examined the legal language of this in such a way that you are aware of any loopholes that are being exploited in this process that seems to be a collaboration between DOJ and the City of New Orleans?

Mr. LANDRY. Well, again, it is concerning that the Department of Justice would go in and basically insert this type of language in a consent decree that had nothing to do with immigration or illegal immigration policies or enforcement of that by local law enforcement in the city. Again, I think that that language frustrates the entire consent decree.

Mr. KING. Would Fire Chief Spencer Chauvin be alive today if we had enforced our immigration laws as intended by this Congress?

Mr. LANDRY. That is correct—I—absolutely. In fact, you can make an argument that everyone who has been a victim or lost a loved one to someone who has been in this country illegally has lost that loved one simply because we fail to enforce existing law.

Mr. KING. Would you disagree with the statement made by Donald Trump several weeks ago that there are thousands of Americans that are grieving today because of the loss of a family member, a loved one due to the failure to enforce immigration law in the United States?

Mr. LANDRY. I do. I agree with that.

Mr. KING. And I would say also, reinforce that, it is thousands. And we have had difficulty in getting apples to apples in two GAO studies. Thank you, Attorney General Landry.

And I would turn to Inspector General Horowitz and just ask you this for clarification. As I listen to your testimony and I read through your testimony, it doesn't come real clear to me as to your position on whether you believe that the sanctuary policy of New Orleans violates 1373.

Mr. HOROWITZ. We looked at the policy that preexisted Friday and found they had a savings clause in their provision, meaning that if—that employees could comply if required to do so by Federal or State law. Our concern was how was that being interpreted and used, because Section 1373 doesn't require anything. It simply prevents state and local jurisdictions and Federal jurisdictions from preventing employees from contacting or responding to ICE——

Mr. KING. Did this policy prevent them from gathering or inquiring as to immigration status?

Mr. HOROWITZ. Parts of the—other parts of the policy did address that.

Mr. KING. And that seems to be the loophole that we have identified over some years here that is exploited by the local jurisdictions.

As my clock ticks down, I would like to, then, ask Ms. Gupta, as you spoke about this, is there any Federal law or any statute that you are aware of that prohibits law enforcement from profiling when they exercise their job?

Ms. GUPTA. Congressman, let me just make one thing clear, if I could, that there is nothing in the NOPD policy that prevents officers from requesting——

Mr. KING. But my question is are you aware of any law or any statute that prohibits profiling in the enforcement of law?

Ms. GUPTA. Yes, there are. The Constitution obviously prevents the racial profiling in the exercise of——

Mr. KING. You mean to say that if there happens to be a white-haired, light-skinned, blue-eyed person that has committed a crime and you are on the hunt for them, you can't say that?

Ms. GUPTA. Where there is a direct and articulated reason, reasonable suspicion, probable cause, these are the——

Mr. KING. Can you characterize the appearance of a suspect in the enforcement of the law?

Mr. GOWDY. The gentleman is out of time, but you may—you may answer.

Ms. GUPTA. Sure. Well, it is against the law to engage in discriminatory policing where——

Mr. KING. Mr. Chairman, I would ask unanimous consent to press this witness until she answers my question. She is evasive in her responses.

Ms. JACKSON LEE. Objection.

Mr. GOWDY. Well——

Ms. JACKSON LEE. The witness has been asked and she has answered.

Mr. KING. She has not answered.

Ms. JACKSON LEE. She has answered the question.

Mr. KING. I would ask unanimous consent for an additional minute.

Ms. JACKSON LEE. Mr. Chairman——

Mr. GOWDY. Well——

Ms. JACKSON LEE [continuing]. She has been asked and she has answered.

Mr. GOWDY. If the gentlelady from Texas would yield, I will address the matter, but——

Ms. JACKSON LEE. I will be happy to yield, sir.

Mr. GOWDY [continuing]. But it is hard for me to interrupt you and do so.

Does the witness feel like she has answered the question as adequately as she is able to do so?

Ms. GUPTA. I do. I am happy to finish the sentence or to yield.

Mr. GOWDY. No. You are welcome to finish the sentence.

Ms. GUPTA. Thank you. Yes, it is illegal and against the law to engage in discriminatory policing, to take policing decisions solely on the basis of one's race or other kind of protected characteristic, yes.

Mr. GOWDY. If the gentleman from Iowa has additional questions, we can entertain a second round.

Mr. KING. I thank the Chairman. And I would just point out that I don't believe I did get an answer to my specific question, but I think it is obvious to the members of the panel. And I would yield back.

Mr. GOWDY. The gentleman from Iowa yields back. The Chair would now recognize the gentlelady from Texas.

Ms. JACKSON LEE. I thank the Chairman very much. And I do want to express my appreciation when any witness comes to share with this lawmaking body, because we should be problem solvers, so let me thank all of you.

I might say that I would join with the comments of my colleagues, that are here on this side of the aisle, and particularly my colleague from New Orleans for his pointed and very responsive questioning, but we should be doing criminal justice reform that I hope that we will do, we should be doing immigration reform, comprehensive immigration reform. And there is a point to the fact that there are cities around the Nation that may need, as you said, Mr. Horowitz, the clarification that I think your pointed inspector general's report has offered us, and I think that is a solution.

So let me first of all ask Ms. Gupta—and thank you again for your service, I don't know where we would be if we did not have the civil rights division, and I thank you so very much. Have you made any pronouncement that New Orleans or any city in the State of Louisiana at this time is not eligible for Federal grants?

Ms. GUPTA. We have not.

Ms. JACKSON LEE. You have made no public statement. Let me read very quickly into the record the genesis of the civil rights division coming to New Orleans. This was a request by Mayor Mitch Landrieu, a request of the U.S. Department of Justice to conduct an investigation. His quote is that, nothing short of complete transformation is necessary and essential to ensure safety for the citizens of New Orleans.

I believe that you are interested in the overall security and safety of all citizens or all individuals in New Orleans. That was the request made by the mayor? Is that my understanding?

Ms. GUPTA. That is right.

Ms. JACKSON LEE. And the representative of the mayor, is that my understanding?

Mr. BUTTERWORTH. That is correct.

Ms. JACKSON LEE. Thank you. I understand that you were looking at the use of excessive force; unconstitutional stop, searches, and arrests; biased policing, including racial and ethnic profiling; and systemic failure to provide effective policing services and systemic failure to investigate sexual assaults and domestic violence. Do you recall that, Ms. Gupta?

Ms. GUPTA. That is right.

Ms. JACKSON LEE. You were overall dealing with the overall civil rights of that community.

So the inspector general offered three points that would help in Section 1373, the clarification, I believe, the—the requiring grant applicants to provide certification about their interaction with ICE, and then ensuring grant recipients clearly communicate to their personnel about 1373.

Do you have any opposition to that?

Ms. GUPTA. No.

Ms. JACKSON LEE. And would you be in compliance or intend to give some guidance to that section?

Ms. GUPTA. Yes. The reason why we made the revisions most recently was to clarify very clearly that the policy complies with 1373, that ICE officer—that NOPD officers can share information regarding the immigration status of an individual with ICE, that there is nothing in NOPD policy that prevents officers from requesting immigration status from ICE as well.

Ms. JACKSON LEE. I just want to be very clear that there is no—there is no ban right now that you have offered and that you are not trying to block. Let me quickly ask this question. I would like to yield to my colleague from New Orleans. Can you tell me if the sentiment expressed by chief manager and the policy of the Major Cities Chiefs Association, in particular, people like Tom Manger, that policies like the one in New Orleans will enhance public safety? Is that something you have heard for other law enforcement agencies, Ms. Gupta?

Ms. GUPTA. Yes. Thank you for the question, Congresswoman. We have heard this from a number of leading law enforcement leaders, but also I think very importantly, the reason why this policy was undertaken was to help the NOPD fight violent crime. When we—in the course of conducting our investigation in New Orleans, we heard from any number of victims and witnesses who were afraid or refusing to cooperate with the NOPD who had critical vital information about crime, and that it was undermining the NOPD's ability to solve and prevent violent crime in those communities.

Ms. JACKSON LEE. Thank you so very much. I am happy to yield to my distinguished colleague from New Orleans, Mr.——

Mr. GOWDY. The gentleman from Louisiana is recognized for 36 minutes—36 seconds.

Mr. RICHMOND. Let me just quickly put the quote that—the great quote that I made in context. It had nothing to do with immigration that Representative King talked about. That quote was because New Orleans was under a Federal consent decree, both the police department and the sheriff's department, and it was costing us over $50 million a year, which was preventing us from making the jail or the police department constitutional.

But since Representative King brought it up, let me just ask you very quickly, Jeff—well, Attorney General Landry, can you please coordinate with the attorney general from Iowa to help them with their 23 sanctuary counties that they have in Iowa, and maybe you can coordinate? Are you willing to coordinate with Representative King to help him with his 23?

Mr. LANDRY. I would be glad to put on a workshop in all 49 other States.

Mr. RICHMOND. Thank you. With that, I yield back.

Ms. JACKSON LEE. Mr. Chairman, I have a submission. I would ask unanimous consent if I might put into the record the following documents: a statement from 11 national civil and immigrant rates—excuse me—rights organizations; statement from the National Immigration Project of the National Lawyers Guild; statement from the National Immigration Forum; statement from Church World Services; statement from 20 law professors, led by Christopher Last; a statement from 17 New Orleans-based community organizations; and a statement from the Law Enforcement Immigration Task Force. I ask unanimous consent to submit these documents into the record.

Mr. GOWDY. Without objection.*

Ms. JACKSON LEE. Thank you. I thank——

Mr. GOWDY. The Chair will now——

Ms. JACKSON LEE. I thank the witnesses. I thank you, Mr. Chairman.

Mr. GOWDY. The Chair will now recognize the gentleman from Colorado, former United States Attorney, Mr. Buck.

Mr. BUCK. Thank you, Mr. Chairman.

Mr. Landry, have you ever prosecuted a case?

Mr. LANDRY. Sir?

Mr. BUCK. Have you ever prosecuted a case?

Mr. LANDRY. A criminal case?

Mr. BUCK. Yes.

Mr. LANDRY. Not since being—not until being attorney general.

Mr. BUCK. Does your office prosecute cases?

Mr. LANDRY. We do.

Mr. BUCK. Mr. Horowitz, did you ever prosecute a case?

Mr. HOROWITZ. I did.

Mr. BUCK. Ms. Gupta, have you ever prosecuted a case?

Ms. GUPTA. My office prosecutes cases, yes.

Mr. BUCK. Okay. And, Mr. Landry, who is your client?

Mr. LANDRY. The State of Louisiana.

Mr. BUCK. The people of the State of the Louisiana?

Mr. LANDRY. That is correct, yes, sir.

Mr. BUCK. Mr. Horowitz, when you prosecuted cases, who was your client?

Mr. HOROWITZ. The people of the United States.

Mr. BUCK. And, Ms. Gupta, when you prosecuted cases, who was your client?

Ms. GUPTA. People of the United States.

Mr. BUCK. Okay. In your opening, Ms. Gupta, you say, police officers—this is the top of page 4 in your written submission, police officers cannot solve crimes and therefore cannot help victims prosecute criminals or help Federal law enforcement deport violent criminals if victims and witnesses feel afraid to share information.

Mr. Landry, why would a victim or witness feel afraid to share information?

Mr. LANDRY. Only because they would be afraid of the suspect.

Mr. BUCK. Okay. Well, how about if they are in this country illegally and they share information and they are asked about their status in this country, would they feel afraid to share information perhaps for that reason? They could be deported or held if they were in the country illegally when they reported a case?

Mr. LANDRY. I believe if a person is victimized, they would be— they would report it regardless of that, but we have seen—look, as a former law enforcement officer, I have seen many communities, especially when you get into the poorer communities, that they are suspect of law enforcement altogether, regardless of their immigration status.

---

*Note: The submitted material is not printed in this hearing record but is on file with the Subcommittee, and can also be accessed at:

http://docs.house.gov/Committee/Calendar/ByEvent.aspx?EventID=105392

Mr. BUCK. Okay. Mr. Horowitz, could someone feel afraid to report a crime because they, in fact, are committing a crime themselves?

Mr. HOROWITZ. It has been a while since I prosecuted a case, but you could certainly see that being a concern of people.

Mr. BUCK. Okay. Well, let's go further, because it has been a while since I prosecuted a case also, so let's dig deep into the recess of our memory here.

Mr. Horowitz, let me ask you something. Is it an allowable part of cross-examination to ask a victim or witness a question that would determine their motive for testifying or reporting a crime?

Mr. HOROWITZ. It is, and obviously depends on the judge's ruling as to the scope of that.

Mr. BUCK. Okay. But your interpretation of law is—the rules of evidence in a broad sense, that would be allowed——

Mr. HOROWITZ. Correct.

Mr. BUCK [continuing]. To question about motive? How about veracity?

Mr. HOROWITZ. That would also be allowed, again, to the extent and scope that the judge allowed it.

Mr. BUCK. Okay. And so if somebody were to report a crime and yet they had committed a crime or they had a motive, for example, a U Visa, if they wanted to stay in the country—you understand what U Visas are. It allows a prosecutor to apply to immigration authorities to allow someone to stay in this country if they are a victim or witness of a crime. It would be fair to inquire of that person whether they had committed a crime themselves by being in the country illegally in order to get a full picture about the prosecutory merits of a case, would it not?

Mr. HOROWITZ. Presumably, but, again, I think it would be, depending on the facts and circumstances, up to the judge ultimately.

Mr. BUCK. Okay. So, Mr. Landry, let me ask you something. When the Department of Justice, the civil rights division, decides that they are going to protect one group of individuals who are committing crimes in this country and make sure that we are not prosecuting another group of individuals, are they in fact choosing which type of criminal they want prosecuted in Louisiana, in New Orleans?

Mr. LANDRY. That is correct. That is exactly. We are choosing between which laws we will follow and which laws we will allow to be broken.

Mr. BUCK. And why would someone do that, politically? What is the political advantage of doing something like that?

Mr. LANDRY. You would have to ask them. I wouldn't engage in that type of activity.

Mr. BUCK. No, you wouldn't, because it is unethical, isn't it?

Mr. LANDRY. That is correct.

Mr. BUCK. If you believe that you are, in fact, not enforcing the laws, or if you enter into a consent decree and you are not representing your client, the people of the United States, the people who are being victimized, that would be unethical conduct, would it not?

Mr. LANDRY. That—it would be.

Mr. BUCK. Mr. Horowitz, do you agree with that?

Mr. HOROWITZ. Depending on the facts and circumstances, yes.

Mr. BUCK. Okay. I yield back.

Mr. GOWDY. The gentleman from Colorado yields back. The Chair would now yield to the gentleman from Texas, the former U.S. Attorney, Mr. Ratcliffe.

Mr. RATCLIFFE. Thank you, Mr. Chairman, for holding this hearing, but I have to confess that I am more than just a little bit embarrassed that the American people have to see a congressional hearing dealing with the absurdity of the subject matter that we are dealing with today.

Right now, Mr. Chairman, at schools across America, we are hopefully teaching our kids about the Constitution. And with all due respect to my colleagues across the aisle, who keep saying that we are hypocritical for asserting that the Federal Government has a role here, I hope we are doing a better job of teaching our kids about the Constitution than we apparently did in teaching some of our colleagues. Because the very first sentence of the Constitution in the preamble is where kids learn that the primary role, the primary role of the Federal Government is to provide for the common defense, and the single-most important part of that is ensuring the sovereignty and integrity of our territorial borders.

Mr. Chairman, that is the reason that we have a Federal Government, that is the one thing that the Federal Government is supposed to do, that is the business the Federal Government is supposed to be in. It is not supposed to be mandating healthcare decisions for Americans, it is not supposed to be interfering with teachers and parents in decisions about kids' education. We have a Federal Government to protect Americans against people from outside our borders who might cause us harm, to protect Americans like Kate Steinle in San Francisco and Spencer Chauvin and Jermaine Starr in Louisiana, and Peter Hacking and Grayson Hacking and Ellie Bryant in my district in northeast Texas, all of whom were killed by illegal aliens who violated the sovereignty and integrity of our territorial borders to come to this country. And, tragically, these are just five of the countless victims killed by illegal aliens every year.

So, Mr. Chairman, if that is the primary role of our Federal Government, if that is why we have a Federal Government, are we really having a hearing about the fact that instead of enforcing our Federal immigration laws, the Federal Government is doing the exact opposite and, as General Landry testified, is actually coercing cities into not complying with Federal immigration laws? And then to add insult to injury, the American people tuning in to this hearing today see that the very same Department of Justice that is tying the hands of law enforcement in places like New Orleans turns around and rewards so-called sanctuary cities by handing out Federal funds even though the conditions for those Federal funds is that the recipients abide by Federal law?

And did I really hear correctly that two-thirds of all Federal money going to law enforcement is going to ten jurisdictions that refuse to comply with Federal immigration laws and that harbor the most violent, violent criminal aliens and refuse to cooperate with the Federal Government to deport them? That, Mr. Chairman, is as shocking as it is shameful.

General Landry, you obviously share my frustration. It is why you wrote to Attorney General Loretta Lynch and asked her whether the Department of Justice, at the same time that they were enthusiastically approving and supporting the New Orleans Police Department policy, was actually also requiring the City of New Orleans to adopt that sanctuary city's policy as part of the consent decree. Did Attorney General Lynch respond to you?

Mr. LANDRY. She finally did respond to me some months later with basically a nonanswer.

Mr. RATCLIFFE. Well, if it makes you feel any better, at least she responded to you. I have written her a lot of letters, and she hasn't responded to any of mine, but we have Ms. Gupta here.

Ms. Gupta, you have heard from Mr. Landry, and I have heard the exchange between you and Mr. Butterworth and Mr. Richmond about really trying to clear up the record here with respect to the fact that this policy is and always was in compliance with Federal law, but as has been pointed out, the record really underscores that it hasn't been, and that is why Congressman Richmond last year in the markup sought to remove that provision to prohibit sanctuary cities from receiving Federal law enforcement grants because of his stated belief that New Orleans would be barred from receiving grants because of immigration provisions in the consent decree.

Ms. Gupta, given that there are legitimate concerns in the NO— in the New Orleans policy by folks here, did you seek a judicial review of the policy by District Court to determine whether or not it complied with Section 1373?

Ms. GUPTA. The District Court at both points, both in February and in issuing this revised policy, had reviewed the policies. Yes.

Mr. RATCLIFFE. Well, my time has expired, but since the attorney general doesn't respond to any of my letters, Ms. Gupta, I wonder if you might carry a message to her, and that message would be on behalf of my constituents and millions of Americans, that if she really believes in enforcing the rule of law, then I think she ought to be prosecuting jurisdictions that violate Federal immigration policy instead of writing them checks.

And with that, I yield back, Mr. Chairman.

Mr. GOWDY. The——

Ms. JACKSON LEE. Mr. Chairman——

Mr. GOWDY [continuing]. Gentleman from Texas yields back. The Chair will now recognize himself.

Mr. Butterworth, what is the penalty for crossing a border unlawfully?

Mr. BUTTERWORTH. I would defer to the Department of Justice on any Federal——

Mr. GOWDY. Well, let's try it this way. Who has exclusive jurisdiction over immigration cases?

Mr. BUTTERWORTH. Again, it is outside of my lane, but I would say it is CBP or ICE.

Mr. GOWDY. So it would be Federal. It is exclusively Federal——

Mr. BUTTERWORTH. Yes, sir.

Mr. GOWDY [continuing]. Both—and they are really—unless you can think of something I can't think of, it is either crossing a border unlawfully or overstaying a visa would be about the only ways you could get in the country unlawfully, only two ways I can think of.

You either cross one of our territorial boundaries or you are invited in and you overstay your visa. And those are both exclusively Federal, but I think you will agree with me that almost all of our interactions in life are with State and local law enforcement. It is not an FBI agent who stops us for speeding. It is not an ATF agent who is working the bar scene. So if most of our citizen police encounters are State and local, and yet immigration is exclusively Federal, how are the Federal officers supposed to know about folks who are not here lawfully.

Mr. BUTTERWORTH. Sir, the Department of Homeland Security has the PEP program, which I am not at liberty to speak on, but I would say if Congress passed a law that commandeered every local police officer and wanted to pay for that, then I think we would welcome it.

Mr. GOWDY. When you saw—well, commandeer is such a pejorative word. How about we just say cooperate? I mean, you don't commandeer people for your terrorism task forces, do you? You don't commandeer people for your narcotics task forces, do you? It is called cooperation.

And yet you have a policy that says that New Orleans Police Department members shall not make inquiries into an individual's immigration status. What do mean by ''inquiries''?

Mr. BUTTERWORTH. Sir, if there is a criminal in New Orleans and an officer interacts with that person and there is a criminal warrant, that person will be——

Mr. GOWDY. See, I don't know what you mean by ''criminal.'' You mean if the person has—if there is probable cause to believe that an offense was committed or if there is already an outstanding warrant?

Mr. BUTTERWORTH. If there is a State, Federal, or local warrant——

Mr. GOWDY. Well——

Mr. BUTTERWORTH [continuing]. Or probable cause that an officer observed conduct that is criminal, they will arrest the person.

Mr. GOWDY. All right. And then they can inquire as to the person's status?

Mr. BUTTERWORTH. Our officers under this policy do not inquire about a person's immigration status.

Mr. GOWDY. They can or cannot?

Mr. BUTTERWORTH. Under this policy, they do not inquire about a person's immigration status.

Mr. GOWDY. Why not?

Mr. BUTTERWORTH. Because we believe that, one, this follows Federal law, and two——

Mr. GOWDY. How are the Federal law enforcement officers supposed to know who is here unlawfully if your officers don't inquire? They are not the ones that are interacting with them. They are not enforcing traffic laws. They don't respond to domestic violence calls. The FBI doesn't have jurisdiction over that; that would be your State and local officers. So how is that supposed to happen?

Mr. BUTTERWORTH. Sir, I think your concerns are with the broader system and not with this policy. In New Orleans, we arrest every criminal that we interact with. We bring them to the jail.

Mr. GOWDY. I love the way you phrase that. You arrest every criminal you interact with. They are only a criminal after they have had a jury trial, Mr. Butterworth. They are a suspect up until that point.

Mr. BUTTERWORTH. Correct.

Mr. GOWDY. Mr. Horowitz, if their original policy was okay, why did they revise it

Mr. HOROWITZ. I don't know the answer to that question, Mr. Chairman. You would have to ask the civil rights division.

Mr. GOWDY. Well, you are a good lawyer, Mr. Horowitz. If the original contract was fine, you usually don't draft another one, unless you just love paying lawyers. I mean, if your original indictment was okay, did you have a superseding indictment?

Mr. HOROWITZ. Generally not.

Mr. GOWDY. No, you don't. So if the original policy is fine, why did we get this brand-new policy?

Mr. HOROWITZ. Well, obviously our memorandum outlining the concerns we had about the provision that then existed may well have triggered the revisions.

Mr. GOWDY. I hate to be cynical, but I think you are right.

Ms. Gupta, you said you were a prosecutor. There was a question I got way back in time that I never really had a good answer for. Whenever a family member who had lost a loved one to an act of violence to someone who was out on bond would ask me, why was that person out of jail? I never really had a good answer. I mean, you can cite the Constitution that you are legally entitled to bond absent some circumstances, but that is kind of a hollow explanation.

So what would the explanation be to those who have lost loved ones to violent crime from people who are here unlawfully and the Federal Government knows it?

Ms. GUPTA. There is, for somebody who has been accused of a violent crime, the NOPD is absolutely entitled in its authority to prosecute to the law to the fullest. And there is nothing in this policy——

Mr. GOWDY. No, no, no. You are either missing my point inadvertently or you are missing my point intentionally. I realize you prosecute people after the homicide. I am trying to figure out how to prevent the homicide. What is the explanation for why the person wasn't dealt with before the murder?

Ms. GUPTA. But, let me just again make clear that the reason we undertook the policy was to ensure that NOPD could fight violent crime could get the kind of critical information from victims and witnesses who need to share critical crime information with the NOPD in order to solve and prevent violent crime and——

Mr. GOWDY. Well, Ms. Gupta, you and I both know that we rely on all sorts of witnesses, some of whom, frankly, expose themselves to criminal liability in the process of cooperating. So the notion that you have to give amnesty to people before they will cooperate with law enforcement has not been my experience.

But, Attorney General Landry, I am out of time. You asked the question. How do you answer it when family members ask you, why was this person not dealt with before they committed the act of violence? I never really had a good answer to that one.

Mr. LANDRY. Unfortunately, I have had to answer that question in Louisiana here lately, and the best way I answer them is that our system in this country is broken.

Mr. GOWDY. With that, I would thank all the witnesses——

Ms. JACKSON LEE. Mr. Chairman, can I ask unanimous consent for 1 minute, please?

Mr. GOWDY. Well, if the gentlelady from Texas does it, then I am sure the gentleman from Texas and the gentleman from Colorado or going to want to do it too.

Ms. JACKSON LEE. Well, let me be very brief, Mr. Chairman.

Mr. GOWDY. Okay. You can have a minute.

Ms. JACKSON LEE. Thank you so very. First of all, I want to make it very clear that I don't think there is one Member here who does not feel the deep pain for the families who have lost loved ones, particularly those who died in the terrible crash trying to help others during the Baton Rouge disaster and flooding. I am from Texas, and I feel for my brothers and sisters in Louisiana and I was there for them in Katrina, so my deepest sympathies.

I do want to make sure, however, General Landry, you are not asking for New Orleans to be prevented from getting Federal funds. Is that correct? You are not asking us to block New Orleans from getting Federal funds?

Mr. LANDRY. I am asking New Orleans to follow Federal law, like I would ask——

Ms. JACKSON LEE. Right. But you are not asking——

Mr. LANDRY [continuing]. All of the citizens of New Orleans.

Ms. JACKSON LEE. I understand, but you are not asking for there to be a declaration for New Orleans not to receive Federal funds from the Department of Justice?

Mr. LANDRY. No. I have been asking for the State to withholds funds from New Orleans for violating Federal law.

Ms. JACKSON LEE. Okay. But let me ask Ms. Gupta. Is New Orleans violating Federal law?

Ms. GUPTA. No. New Orleans under this policy, the policy does not violate Federal law. And right now we are working with the City of New Orleans to ensure constitutional policing.

Ms. JACKSON LEE. That they are communicating with ICE and you are not blocking that, because that is what I want to make sure is happening.

Ms. GUPTA. That is right. The policy makes clear that NOPD can communicate with ICE and request information from ICE about a person's immigration status and citizenship.

Ms. JACKSON LEE. And deal with criminal——

Mr. GOWDY. The gentlelady's time has expired.

Ms. JACKSON LEE. Thank you so very much for your service, all of you. Thank you.

Mr. GOWDY. With that, I would thank all four of our witnesses.

Members are advised they will have 5 legislative days to submit additional materials to the record.

With that, I thank you again to the four witnesses. And we are adjourned.

[Whereupon, at 12:08 p.m., the Subcommittee was adjourned.]